This book is dedicated to
Mary . . .
Melinda . . .
and
Maria . . .
. . . who taught me the necessity
of money management.

A COMPLETE GUIDE TO THE CHRISTIAN'S BUDGET

MICHAEL L. SPEER

BROADMAN PRESS/NASHVILLE, TENNESSEE

Library of Congress Catalog Card Number: 74-80341
Dewey Decimal Classification: 640
Printed in the United States of America

CONTENTS

INTRODUCTION

Let me begin this book with a confession—I have problems managing my money! Don't we all? The problem of managing our money will be with us all of our lives. Perhaps that is a startling thought. Think about it. Money management is not an option. We do not have any choice about whether or not to manage our money. Our only choice is between effective and ineffective management.

For the Christian, a special responsibility is connected with the family budget and money management. As with other resources, the Christian should understand that money belongs to God—he is owner, of both possessions and the possessor, of us and all our resources. God simply allows us to *use* what he owns. God is the owner—man is the trustee. It is this understanding that makes budgets and the use of our money of particular importance to the Christian. He sees his responsibility to care for God's things and his mission to multiply God's things for God's glory.

Inflation, excess credit buying, and the constant desire for more and more "things" are the villains that cause most American families to feel a financial pinch. During times of spiraling inflation, we must each strive to make the most of every available dollar.

Although proper money management will not guarantee

wealth, it will mean more happiness and a better attitude toward all of life. For most of us the problem is not so much the amount of money we earn as it is how we use what we have. All of us want to get the most value out of each dollar and build a secure financial future for our families. By adhering to principles of good economizing and conservation, as Christian stewards, we can continue to provide adequately for our families, contribute to the national good, and still support the expanding and urgent ministries of our local churches and mission ministries around the world.

This book is written in an attempt to help Christians confront every area of their budget and examine it in the light of biblical precepts. A budget should be recognized as a tool to help give direction to achieving family goals. It should be a general plan for organized spending, giving, and saving. A budget isn't just for cutting down, although it may help to do that when cutting down is necessary. It should reveal ways to afford more of life's good things and allow you to demonstrate your Christian commitment more fully. A good budget should be tailored to fit *your* living and *your* wishes. With the support of the entire family it can lead to spending that is more purposeful and meaningful.

If you have a dream for the future you should remember that the future is not some far off point in time when all of those dreams will come true. Your future starts right now. Only you can take the necessary steps to shape that future. It is for you that this book is written. It is offered with the hope that it will provide some additional insights into an area of life which requires careful and prayerful commitment.

Michael L. Speer

1.
IN
THE
BEGINNING . . .
(Building the Foundation)

There's only one place to start—at the beginning! When you build a house, you can't put the roof on first. You must begin with the foundation. Any discussion about budgets and the use of our possessions must also start with a foundation. There's no use talking about budgets, saving, giving, or planning for the future unless you have a solid foundation on which to build.

"In the beginning God" (Gen. 1:1). Before anything else was, God was. Then God did something—he "created." God created the heaven and the earth and all that is in them. He created the sun, the moon, and the stars. He furnished the earth elaborately with the right kind of atmosphere, elements, animal life, resources, and a beautiful garden. Then he created man, and man was just right for his world. He could breathe the air, live off the earth's resources, enjoy the beautiful surroundings, and have fellowship with God. God entrusted all material things to man.

Most of us take our material possessions for granted. We give little thought to the religious meaning of things and their place in our lives and destinies. It is important for the Christian to answer such questions as: Why did God create the world? What is the role of material things in the life of man? What is the proper relation of man to the world of things?

The Creation of All Things

When we think about the creation of things, our minds turn to Genesis 1-2. Here the creation story is presented in two parts: 1:1-3 and 2:4-25. These two accounts are separate and sometimes even seem contradictory. They are different in emphasis. The first is oriented more toward God and heaven, while the second is oriented toward man and the earth. Although they are different in style, language, and representation, the teaching of both is basically the same.

As the story unfolds, we are given the order followed by God in his creative activity. God progresses from the simple to the more complex, from the lower to the higher forms. Each work of creation is complete within itself and has its own function. At the same time, it is related to the other systems and to the whole.

The creative work of God reaches a climax in the creation of man. Man is formed from clay. There is a close bond between man and the earth. In Genesis 1:22 and 28, the blessing, the command to multiply, and the granting of plant life for food unite man with the animal world. Man is a part of the rest of creation. But at the same time, he is apart from the rest of creation. Man is unique in that he is the only part of creation made in the image of God. He is uniquely related to God and has a unique responsibility to God.

When God surveyed the work of creation, he was pleased. Five times the statement appears, "And God saw that it was good." There is a significant variation in the final statement, "And God saw everything that he had made, and, behold, it was very good" (Gen. 1:31). God's creation was "completely perfect"—a world characterized by beauty, purity, and harmony. All created things were good in themselves in relation to the purposes of God.

As a part of this "good" creation, man has a representative function on earth. He is responsible for the working out of God's will and is responsible to God for the response he makes. He is to be a trustee of material possessions and use them for the purpose of God. He is to use them for the glory of God and the good of his fellowman.

Man's basic attitude toward his responsibility both to God and to his fellowman should be one of joy. Man should take great delight in his work. The joy of man is a central emphasis in both the Old and New Testaments.

The Role of Things in the Life of Man

The Bible teaches that the material world is essential to man's life. It is necessary for the sustenance of the body and for the stability of the mind and emotions. Man's dependence on the world of things is a part of the purpose of God. All things belong to God. He either created them or gives the power to make them. He gives them in love and expects them to be used in accordance with his purpose.

God's material gifts are to be enjoyed by all. God expects both people and possessions to be used according to his purpose. When we betray this divine trust, we lose the good life. Man's sin affects not only man himself, but also his surroundings. Punishment is the inevitable consequence of man's sin. Two dramatic illustrations of the close connection between man and things in sin and judgment are given in the curse placed on Cain (Gen. 4:1-12) and in the story of the flood (Gen. 6:5-7).

God created things to serve the needs of man, the focal point of his purpose. All the rest of creation was less than man, and was created for his good. When man sinned against God, he was alienated from God and his environment. Redemption was necessary if God's ultimate purpose was to be achieved. God's plan of salvation began in the election of Israel. This was first made known in the call of Abraham and confirmed in the Exodus and the making of the covenant. A part of this plan was the gift of the land to the people of God.

The patriarchs had God's promise that he would give them the land of Canaan, but the title remained in God's name. The Israelites had temporary ownership, but they were forbidden to sell the land permanently. The security and prosperity of the people were dependent upon their love and loyalty to God. If they rebelled against God, they would lose the land. Just as the possession of the land was their prime blessing, so its loss was to be their prime punishment.

Today "the land" still belongs to God. Although things have been entrusted to us, no matter how we use them or abuse them, God's title is valid even after ours has expired.

The Christian Meaning of Ownership

The next step in building our foundation is to consider what the Bible says about our use of the good gifts that God has placed in our trust. What should be the Christian's attitude toward ownership? How should the Christian use his possessions? These questions are basic to our understanding.

People are property-minded. We take great pride in our possessions. We live in an age in which things are produced on a scale never before known. Most of our time is spent acquiring things. We are concerned about making a living, providing for our families, and preparing for the future. If we are not careful, our desire for things may become so great that it will lead us to selfishness and a callous attitude toward others.

A man bought a new lawnmower. His neighbor asked if he might use it. The man answered: "Certainly, use it all you like. There is one condition, though—I never permit it to be used away from my home!" The man was exercising a right of ownership. He was the owner; he had the right to decide how his property was to be used! We belong to God. God has the right to determine how his property is to be used.

The above attitude toward ownership follows closely the pattern of ancient Rome, which was neither God-centered nor concerned with man's responsibility for the needs of others. This test of ownership is not based on the right to use and enjoy possessions; rather, it seems to be the right of the owner to keep any other person from using them. We may purchase something and have a clear title to it and never use it or enjoy it. But if someone else needs it and tries to take it, he is considered a thief.

The dangers inherent in the idea that exclusive use is the distinguishing mark of ownership need to be reviewed. In such a concept, selfishness is apparent. This truth is illustrated in the parable of the good Samaritan (Luke 10:30-37). The good Samaritan demonstrated the ideal attitude toward ownership for the Christian. He seemed to be saying, "What I have is yours if you need it. I will gladly share with you in your need." This spirit of sharing was strong among the early Christians.

In the New Testament, the right of ownership was accepted. Jesus visited the home of Mary, Martha, and Lazarus. He never condemned them for their ownership of property. He spoke of a man buying a field and of a merchant finding a priceless pearl and selling everything he had to buy the newfound treasure. The rich young ruler was told to sell his possessions because of his attitude toward his property—not as a condemnation of ownership.

Christian ownership means that Christ owns the things a Christian possesses. It is man's stewardship of God's ownership.

The Christian Use of Things

It has been said that "man cannot live by bread alone," but neither can he live without bread! Christians face the problem of appreciating the good things God has made without becoming slaves of these good things.

Determining the Christian use of things requires a fine sense of balance. The Christian use of things is rooted in his understanding of the purpose of life. This includes the provision for our necessities as well as a reasonable provision against the hazards of life. We are challenged to use our possessions for our own enrichment and the blessing of others. There also should be a balance between spending for ourselves and what is given for kingdom causes.

Three uses of possessions which are clearly founded on biblical practice and teaching are the support of oneself and one's dependents, aid to the less fortunate, and support for the ministry.

First, the Christian must provide for his necessities and for those dependent on him. Jesus taught us to pray for "our daily bread," for the physical necessities of life. Some people in Thessalonica expected an immediate return of Christ. They used this as an excuse to quit work. Paul said that if any did not work, they should not eat (2 Thess. 3:10).

Second, there is no question about the Bible's supporting the use of possessions to help the unfortunate who do not have the necessities of life. In the Old Testament specific provisions were made to care for the poor. They were allowed to glean in the fields (Lev. 19:9-10). They had the first right to sabbatical fruits (Ex. 23:11). The third year tithe was for the benefit of the poor and needy (Deut. 14:28-29; 26:12).

Finally, the Bible supports the use of possessions to carry on the ministry. In Israel provision was made for the subsistence of the Levites by the people's tithe (Lev. 27:32-33). In the New Testament, the support of the preaching ministry has its roots in the teaching and preaching of Jesus (Mark 6:8-11).

Many Christians emphasize the first use of possessions—the support of self and dependents. Throughout the New Testament

Jesus seems to be saying, "Don't get entangled with worry over the necessities of life and miss the *purpose* of life." We have our commission to go into all the world with the gospel of Christ. The sharing of our individual and corporate possessions makes this possible. It allows each of us to have a daily share in ministering to the needs of others and supporting those whose lives have been dedicated to ministering.

The Christian Life-Style

With a solid foundation of biblical understanding of the role of material possession in the life of a Christian, it is important to answer the question, What should be the Christian's life-style?

A small child doesn't cry over the length of a hemline. But if that child is a girl, the length of her dress will be extemely important to her later in life. The style of clothing matters to most people. This has long been true for women, and now they are being challenged by men to see who can have the most colorful clothes and the best hair styles.

A style of living can bring admiration. "Nathan really knows how to live!" This statement probably means that he drives a sharp car, is married to a beautiful wife, has a cabin on the lake, or peels off his money from a wad of bills.

But back to the small child. He could care less about style. He only cares about himself. Style is something he has to learn to appreciate. He is self-centered. He gets hungry and wants something to eat, and he yells until he gets it. His first vocabulary is composed of words like *me, mine, get, I,* and *want.* Give me *my* toy. You can't play with *my* ball. I want *my* candy.

A child has to be taught about God, about how he should live. We all have to be taught about the life-style of a Christian.

Perhaps you are asking, What does all of this have to do with a Christian budget? Everything! Some people grow up without being taught. They have no foundation on which to build a purpose in life. But an understanding of what Christ expects of us in relation to the use of our possessions is basic to everything we do. We might call this an understanding of the concept of "calling."

In the Old Testament, calling is basically corporate, for the group, as God called a nation to be his people. This community, God's people, in the Old Testament is Israel. In the New Testament, this community is the fellowship of believers, God's new people. Thus, all of the community of believers, all of God's people, are "called." We are called to have a single vocation—to follow Christ in discipleship.

This calling to follow Christ in discipleship, in mission and ministry, is the very heart of Christian stewardship. God has called all of his people to be stewards of all they possess.

One man said that as he turned his life over to the lordship of Christ and discovered the demands of discipleship, he suddenly realized that his house, his possessions, and his occupational skills belonged to Christ literally, and that they were to be used in trust to accomplish Christ's mission.

Because of this view of calling, a person's life takes on new meaning. The person's attitude toward possessions and their use is changed because of his understanding of calling to be involved with Christ in his mission and ministry in the world.

The Christian life-style is an expression of that calling to follow Christ in discipleship. It may be defined as the believer's *inner* relationship to God finding expression in his *outward* relationship to things. It is an expression of ministry and mission for that person. It is a way to live out the meaning of what discipleship is all about.

The really crucial decision comes, *not* when a person decides that he will give a tithe of his income to his church this year rather than give his usual ten dollars a week, but when this man, understanding the claim of Christ on all of life and his surrender to discipleship, *seeks to be responsible for all he possesses.* Whether that leads him to give a tithe or 50 percent is wholly secondary, for he has learned what it means to be a good steward. He has begun to seek to express stewardship as a life-style that is consistent with his understanding of the biblical teaching about the calling of all of God's people in discipleship.

A person who has caught this vision of stewardship looks out on the world and tries to see how its needs can be matched by his own ability to be a good steward of possessions. Deciding to be a good steward, he takes seriously his discipleship; and that is exactly what he ought to do. He believes that this is God's world, and he is trying to find a way to be a responsible disciple to Christ through a stewardship of all he has. This becomes his life-style.

Just as a child must be taught, so must each of us be open to an understanding of God's purpose for our material possessions. Jesus made one of the most crucial statements regarding the Christian life-style at the conclusion of the long passage on the subject in the Sermon on the Mount: "But seek ye first the kingdom of God, and his righteousness; and all these things shall be added unto you" (Matt. 6:33).

There is a "first" and there is an "all these things." Here the old saying, "Put first things first," is not quite good enough. The New Testament makes it evident that the "first" of which Jesus speaks is a singular and not a plural. Therefore, we would have to say "put the first thing first." Put God's will first in your life and everything else will take care of itself.

The most important decision that anyone ever makes is the decision to make Jesus Christ the Lord of *all* of life. That's the foundation—that's the beginning.[1]

For Your Consideration

1. *Why did God create things?*
2. *What should be the role of things in the life of man?*
3. *What is the proper relation of man to the world of things?*
4. *What should be the Christian attitude toward ownership?*
5. *How should the Christian use his possessions?*
6. *What do we mean by "calling"?*
7. *What do we mean by "life-style"?*

Notes

1. The material in this chapter is from two basic sources:

Resource Unlimited, edited by William L. Hendricks, 1972, SBC Stewardship Commission, Nashville, Tennessee.

Source, October-December 1973, Unit 2, "Developing Christian Stewardship," Michael L. Speer (articles). Most of this information was also from *Resource Unlimited*.

2.
YOUR ATTITUDE IS IMPORTANT

(Serving God with Mammon)

We were head over heels in debt. Inflation, charge accounts, and unexpected medical bills had us at an all time low. I had just picked up a $63 repair bill on our roof, when my wife, Mary, announced that Ruth's coat simply wouldn't last another winter. To make matters even worse, I had just come from the garage where the mechanic had told me that our old car needed $115 worth of work to keep it going.

My spirits hit bottom. I said facetiously, "Oh, well, it's only money." Mary looked at me as though I was crazy—then both of us began to laugh.

"You're right," she said, "it's only money. That's not very important compared to things like friends, happiness, health, and our children. We've worried so much that we've lost our perspective."

"It's only money" has become a familiar phrase in our family ever since. When some unexpected expenses knock the top out of our budget, we keep our minds on our blessings rather than on our problems. Of course, we do everything we can to cope with the problem and work it out, but we try to keep smiling as we assure ourselves, "It's only money."

A story quite different from this is told of a young man who found a five dollar bill on a parking lot one day. He became so elated over his good fortune that he never stopped looking for lost money. Over a period of 40 years he found 70 pennies, 21 dimes, 29,473 buttons, and 56,231 pins. As a result of his search, his posture became stooped, and he developed a miserly disposition.

Which of the stories could be *your* story? Neither, I hope. Your attitudes probably lie somewhere between the two, but the fact remains that it is often difficult for us to develop the proper attitudes toward money. Christians have a particular responsibility in this area.

What Money Is and What It Represents

Money is important to people! And, conversely, people are important to money. How we use money determines whether it gains power to create or to destroy. Money in itself is only a tool of man. Whether it is used for good or evil depends on the person and not on the coin. It is often said that money is the root of all evil. But Paul said that "the *love* of money" is one of the roots of evil (1 Tim. 6:10). Paul puts the responsibility where it should be—on the person, not on the system of exchange.

Before we can develop proper attitudes toward money, it is essential that we understand just what money is and what it represents. The dictionary tells us that it is standard pieces of gold, silver, copper, nickel, etc., stamped by government authority or any paper note issued by a government or an authorized bank and used as a medium of exchange.

In primitive days, a system of exchange was used called "barter." This was simply an exchange of goods or property by one owner with another for something of equal value. In more recent days, this practice has been refined to the point that we can "sell" our valuable possessions, including time, labor, or skills, for what we call "money." We then exchange this money for other necessities and luxuries of life. In our age of advanced technology we are quickly coming to the place where money will be just as out of date as the barter system is. In the near future, machines may handle our transactions without our ever actually handling any money. Earnings will automatically be deposited in our bank. When we make a purchase, our own personalized card will be inserted into a machine that will automatically transfer a certain amount of credit from our account to that of the one from whom we are making the purchase. Money, as such, will then become virtually obsolete, but some system of accounting will be maintained.

Benjamin Franklin said: "Money never made a man happy yet, nor will it. There is nothing in its nature to produce happiness. The use of money is all the advantage there is in having it." [1]

In light of this, consider what money represents rather than what it is. Money represents stored-up life or personality. It has been called "coined personality" and "congealed sweat." It is the medium through which men exchange their abilities, their labor, their skills, and their ingenuity.

A definition of money for our purpose is simply this: Money is myself. I am a working man. I hire myself out for a week at $40 a day. At the end of the week I get $200, and I put it in my pocket or in the bank. What is that $200? It is one week's worth of my work. It represents a part of me!

When a Christian begins to understand this, he begins to understand that the money in his pocket is not merely silver and gold, but it represents something human. It is a part of life itself. When we spend, we are spending a part of our lives. But when we give, it becomes even more meaningful because we are giving back to our Lord a part of our stored self. [2]

Our Responsibility for Possessions

For the Christian, money is important for a particular reason, and a special responsibility is connected with the management of money. As with other resources, the Christian understands that money belongs to God—he is owner, of both possessions and the possessor, of us and all our resources. God simply allows us to *use* what he owns. God is owner—man is a trustee. It is this understanding that makes the use of money of particular importance to the Christians. He sees his responsibility to care for God's things and his mission to multiply God's things for God's glory.

The Christian steward has found great joy and peace of mind from the realization that money is to be used according to God's purposes and that he should determine the use of all his possessions on the basis of how that particular resource can be used according to God's particular purpose. The Christian steward values his relationship to God as his greatest treasure and actually derives more benefit from the things he possesses and infinitely more from all the life.

Test your attitude toward money matters by placing a check mark in the appropriate space below:

	Yes	No
1. Do you lose the joy in life experiences when you are denied material comforts?	—	—
2. Are you willing to hazard the life and health of yourself or your family to secure more money or material possessions?	—	—
3. Does your job keep you from having time to serve Christ?	—	—
4. Would you accept a job you did not enjoy simply because it "paid more money"?	—	—
5. Do you argue often about money matters in your home?	—	—
6. Do you try to make all the money you can because money represents power, security, and freedom?	—	—
7. Are you frequently afraid that people will take advantage of you in money matters?	—	—

8. Do you spend money for things you want now
   rather than save for long-range goals?   ___ ___

If you answered yes to one or more of the questions, perhaps
it is time to reevaluate your attitude toward money matters.

Acquiring Possessions

Another important factor for the Christian steward is that
he pursue God's purpose and reflect Christ's control in his life
in acquiring possessions. He believes that all services and voca-
tions are honorable if they are honestly chosen and pursued
for the good of men and the glory of God. In choosing his
work, the Christian will immediately eliminate certain types of
work. He will not choose anything that is wrong in itself or
that is harmful to mankind or that would hinder his witness
for Christ. He will not consider anything that would injure people
physically, mentally, socially, morally, or spiritually; anything
that would make it more difficult for people to live right and
do good. The Christian will demand that his work call for a
respect of man's dignity and worth in relationship to earning.
He will be more concerned with the greater value of honesty
in his work than he is in the dollars he earns. He will require
that the manner of earning be God-honoring.

In his letter to the Philippians (Phil. 1:27-30), Paul emphasized
that no matter what happened to him or to them, they must
live worthily of their faith in God. The Authorized Version says:
"Let your conversation be as it becometh the gospel of Christ."
Actually, this is rather misleading. To us the word "conversation"
means "talk"; but in the seventeenth century, when this version
was translated, the word "conversation" meant one's conduct
or behavior. It was the person's whole way of life that counted.
The phrase literally means: "Let your entire behavior be worthy
of one who calls himself a Christian."

Paul reminded the people that even though they lived in a colony, far from Rome, they still lived and acted as Romans were expected to. Then he emphasized that they had an even greater duty than that. He reminded them that wherever they were they must live as a citizen of the kingdom of God, never forgetting the privileges and responsibilities of that citizenship.

The world is full of Christians who, when Christianity is difficult, conceal or at least play down their Christianity. But the true Christian remains faithful regardless of the company, the place, or the business circumstances.

The ultimate purpose of all work should be to serve the Lord. This gives life its true meaning and makes of it a means to a worthy end. What is your attitude toward your work? Can you truthfully make each of the following statements?

My work is satisfying to me personally.

My work is useful to society.

My work expresses my freedom and not my bondage.

My work is a witness to the world of the Christian meaning and value of work.

My work reflects my commitment to following the call of discipleship.

What Jesus Said About Attitudes

A Christian's attitude toward all of his possessions is very important. Jesus was certainly no lover of money. He never owned a home. He never received a salary. He would not be considered successful by the standards many now use to measure achievement. But he was very much concerned that people have the right attitude toward things and that people possess things and not be possessed by them. He was aware that the wrong sense of relationship to material possessions could eliminate the effectiveness of a life and could create great problems in a person's spiritual influence.

Jesus had more to say about man's attitude toward his possessions than any single theme which he discussed. In sixteen of his thirty-eight parables Jesus made man's attitude toward money his theme. He called a man a "steward" of his possessions. In the society of New Testament times, a steward held a position of honor and dignity. He was one who managed the possessions of another. Jesus took the idea of stewardship and used it to express the relationship between man and God and the attitude which man should have toward the purpose for all material things.

Jesus talked about money because he saw its potential for good or evil depending on our attitude toward it. He saw what it could do to people and for people. He gave us a vital message when he said, "He who is faithful with a trifle is also faithful with a large trust" (Luke 16:10, Moffatt). And then in the next verse he partially explained what he meant by adding, "So if you are not faithful with dishonest mammon, how can you ever be trusted with true riches?"

Jesus also taught that money which was not consecrated to God was a blight on a person's spiritual life. He was sorrowed over the rich young man, not because he had great possessions, but because the great possessions had him. "How difficult it is," he exclaimed, "for those who have money to enter into the kingdom of God!" Of course, it would be wrong of us to think that Jesus was talking only about rich men. Most rich men were poor at one time, and most poor men covet the rich man's money. Someone has said, "When a man begins to make money, God either gains a new fortune or loses a soul." Life is often proof of this.

Jesus' emphasis on attitudes toward material things and the use we should make of them is pointed up in his description of the poor widow who gave money away, the rich fool who hoarded his possessions, the prodigal son who squandered his money, and the rich young man who worshiped it. Jesus realized that a man's basic attitude toward material things determines his attitude toward the rest of life.

Again and again Jesus confronted men with the question, "What will a man be profited, if he gains the whole world, and forfeits his soul?" (Matt. 16:26, NASB). On another occasion he said, "A man's life consisteth not in the abundance of the things which he possesseth" (Luke 12:15, KJV). He was really saying through this, that man is of value primarily because of the reach of his soul and his relationship with God, not because of what he has.

In his book *The Christian in the Modern World*, T. B. Maston says of Jesus' statement, "Come ye after me" (Mark 1:17): "Jesus was interested primarily in men and invited them to follow him not because of what he might get from them but because of what he might do for them and what they in turn might do for the kingdom of God.

"Jesus today is primarily interested in us personally and not in what we have. It may cost us something to respond to his call, but if we follow him we shall be amply repaid."

A person's attitude, rather than his circumstances, usually determines his general financial stability. Money is our medium of exchange, and the way we earn it and our use of it give evidence of what we believe is really important.

Because of our relationship to God through Jesus Christ, Christians have the responsibility of developing right attitudes toward money. Neither shrugging it off with "It's only money" nor hoarding it is the proper attitude.

The proper attitude can only be developed as we understand what money is in the light of God's creation of material goods and Jesus' teachings concerning possessions.

For Your Consideration

1. *What does money represent to you?*
2. *Why should money be important for a particular reason for the Christian?*
3. *What do we mean by a "steward"?*
4. *What factors should a Christian consider related to his work?*
5. *What should be the ultimate purpose of all work?*
6. *What did Jesus say about man's attitude toward possessions?*
7. *How can we develop proper attitudes toward money and our material possessions?*

Notes

1. "Stewardship Facts 1966-67, "National Council of the Churches of Christ in the U.S.A., 475 Riverside Drive, New York, New York 10027.

2. *Baptist Adults*, May 25, 1969, Session 1, "Man and His Money," by Michael L. Speer. (The entire first section of this chapter is taken from this article.)

3.
WHY AND HOW TO BUILD A BUDGET
(Buy That Dream)

A man and his wife in Kentucky went to a financial counselor. His plea went something like this: "Please help us get out of the financial whirlpool that we've been in for the most of the eight years that we've been married. When we got married, we expected to have all of the things that our parents had, although they had worked almost a lifetime to accumulate them. We plunged in too deep and have never gotten out. Our problem has always been the same. We have debts that are practically impossible to pay but must be paid. We no sooner get one thing taken care of, until we find that something else is presenting a problem. We've simply transferred the load from one finance company to another. When we got married, we were both working and making nearly $9,000 a year. When the children came along my wife stopped working. Doctor and hospital bills, increased costs for food and clothing, the need for a larger home, and inflation have simply driven us deeper into debt. When this happens we find ourselves using installment buying and finally, back to the finance company. If there's an answer we haven't found it. We're drowning in debt. What can we do?"

Problems with Money Management

Does this sound familiar? In our land where jobs are plentiful, it seems to be easier to earn money than it is to manage it wisely. Soaring inflation makes it doubly important and increasingly difficult. Surveys indicate that more people worry about money than any other single problem. The American Consumer's Guide, *How to Get More for Your Money*, states: "There are many reasons why marriages break up. Prominent among them are grave problems with money. A recent study of requests for help made to family service agencies shows that more than half the couples who asked for counseling reported serious disputes over money. The book *A Guide to Successful Family Living* by the general directors of the Family Service Association of America, Clark W. Blackburn and Norman M. Lobenz, state: 'How a couple manages money can often be a key to the health of the marriage; every couple should have some kind of mutually agreed-upon plan for handling finances.' " [1]

The problem of worrying about money is true whether the income is $5,000 or $50,000. No matter what you think, it is not merely a matter of income. You will find that each level of income has its own pattern, its own narrow range of freedom. The problem is not so much the amount of money we earn, as it is how we use it. All of us are interested in handling money successfully. We want to get the most value out of each dollar and build a secure financial future for our families. For the Christian, it is imperative. The primary goal of the Christian family is known more by the way it handles its money than by any other practice. The way we use money is a demonstration of what we believe is important. It is a testimony to our life-style. For this reason, the Christian family has a particular responsibility to manage its money wisely. It is important to have a plan for spending, giving, and saving, and to try to follow that plan.

The problem of managing your income will be with you all of your life. Some people handle the problem well and live comfortably and relatively free from money worries. They derive pleasure and real satisfaction from the use of all their possessions. Others dive in too deeply and never get out of the whirlpool. Most of us work hard for our money and should be willing to make a sincere effort to see that it is managed and used wisely. Never before in history has there been such mass affluence, with so many families making so much money. However, many of these American families feel financially pinched rather than feeling rich. This is partially true because of increased taxes and inflation. For example, if your income increased by 50 percent or less from 1966 to 1974, your take-home pay actually buys less than it did before, in spite of the fact that you are earning more. The villains are local, state, and federal taxes, including raising Social Security costs, and inflation, which has eroded the 1966 dollar down to only about 55 percent of its buying power in 1974.[2] The constant desire for more and more "things" and excess credit buying are other villains. These will be discussed in chapter 4, "Getting in and out of Debt." Therefore, if you can learn the secret of controlling your family income, it may be possible to stretch your money by 10 percent, 20 percent, or even more.

The Importance of Good Money Management

Money management is not an option. The choice is not "to manage or not to manage." The choice is between effective and ineffective management. Although proper money management will not guarantee wealth, it will mean more happiness and a better attitude toward all of life. Remember, too, that money can do more than purchase material possessions. It can do much to make life meaningful and worth living. Money given to support the ministries of your church, or spent for a concert or family trip, will enrich your living, although it does not add to your material possessions.

Money management is related to objectives and goals. It is related to the things we believe and the things we hope to achieve. It has to do with both the present and the future. We cannot go back and change what we did yesterday, but yesterday's experiences can provide a valuable background for tomorrow. We can develop a plan to more effectively manage the resources we have today, and we can plan to manage more effectively the resources we hope to have tomorrow.

This chapter is mainly concerned with family money management, although planning for single people is not much different and most of the same rules apply. One great problem which families have that single people don't is that a family's spending and saving plan must include the loyalty of all family members and must satisfy every one as being fair. This calls for family cooperation, agreement, and willingness to change the plan from time to time to meet the changing family needs.

Too often the purpose of a money management plan, or budget, is misunderstood. It is not a tool to reduce you to servitude, but rather one to bring you greater freedom. It is not hard-and-fast lines, but is a flexible guide to give direction in family spending. It is a general plan for organized spending, giving, and saving drawn up in advance, not a record of expenditures set down afterward. A budget isn't just for cutting down, although it may help to do that when cutting down is necessary. It should reveal ways to afford more of life's good things and allow you to demonstrate your Christian commitment more fully. It can lead to spending that is more purposeful and meaningful.

Have you ever said to yourself: "Look at all the money we have spent this year. What in the world have we done with it? What do we have to show for it?" If you really want to know what has happened to your money, it might be interesting and helpful to stop and take inventory of the things you bought beyond the necessities with the money you have earned during the past few years. Whatever these things were, you should remember that they seemed to be worthwhile at the time you bought them. They were something you just had to have. Take a pencil and make an honest list. Suppose you call it "Last Year's Dreams."

List them one by one and approximately how much each cost you. The list will probably include some things that are no longer around. This means an investigation of your way of living, as well as a search for what happened to your earnings.

You will probably discover that several of these "old dreams" failed to measure up to the dollars you paid for them. When you realize the total cost of these, you may be surprised. But don't be too disheartened. When you finish "Last Year's Dreams," try making another list. This will provide much more satisfaction. Make a list of those things which you bought that brought a great deal of satisfaction. These were worth every penny you spent for them. Both these lists are important because, when you are considering a new purchase, they may help you to remember to wait long enough to compare the cost with some old purchase you made which proved to be either "costly" or "cost-worthy."

The Necessity of a Plan

If you are honest and thorough about an examination of your past spending, it will lead you to a wholesome, searching question: "What do I really consider important for my family and myself?" This is the question that many people have never discovered an answer for. But the answer is there if you are willing to look. A wise plan of money management is necessary. It's not magic, but it can certainly go a long way toward making those current and future "dreams" become a reality. It is probably true that the fundamental problem of most families in financial difficulty is the fact that they didn't "want" enough. Having no great purpose, they were easy targets for all the petty trifles which were dangled before their eyes every day. They simply didn't dare to dream.

If you really want to have something to show for those hard-earned dollars, you must plan in advance exactly what you want and need. Then use the money for those things before it disappears in unexpected ways. Remember that your future is not some far-off point in time when all of your dreams will come true. It starts right now, and you must take the necessary steps to shape that future.

If this is your first try at money management, set up a trial plan. After you see how your budget works, you can revise it, if necessary, to cover a longer period. If your earnings are quite low, you will need to plan more carefully to take care of your immediate needs and current bills. If your earnings are irregular, base your estimate on your previous year's income and your current prospects.

A good budget should be tailored to fit *your* living and *your* wishes. It is impossible to base a budget on the standards of some imaginary "average" family, or on percentages of income which that average family might spend on contributions, food, clothing, shelter, and transportation. The number in your family, your income, the type of work you do, your talents, interests, the neighborhood and part of the country in which you live—all of these influence your desires and spending needs. What talents in the family should be encouraged and made an important part of your plans? Where do you want to be in five years? How do you want to live? What contribution do you want to make to your church?

A good plan, drawn with confidence and courage and with the support of the entire family, can change your lives. The very existence of such a plan sets you apart as a family who sits at the controls rather than one just going along for the ride.

Planning-can also help make your family a team. There may easily be more dollar advantage from achieving family cooperation than from a raise in pay. Planning and working together for something as a family group will eliminate several problems at once. It will make many of the things which have been draining off your income seem very unimportant when compared to the main goals. It will teach your children something of the value of money, and it will help to give them a sense of purpose.

Basic Causes of Financial Problems

In considering guidelines for building your budget, it is well to be aware of the three basic reasons why families get into financial difficulty. The primary reason is the failure to set anything aside for an emergency fund. Each family should determine how much will be needed and begin setting something aside regularly for that purpose until the desired amount is reached. It is a good rule to provide enough to cover expenses for two to three months without other income. It is also well to have enough insurance so that a death, disability, or major illness will not completely shatter the family's future.

Second, there is the temptation to budget more than the *net* take-home pay. Remember that the amount deducted for taxes, retirement, hospitalization, and other such items cannot be considered as available income. Of course if a deduction is for life insurance or medical coverage, it is a payment towards your family protection. If it is for a retirement program, annuity, or the purchase of savings bonds or stock certificates, it is an investment in your family's savings. Some payroll deductions are set by law while you can adjust others upwards or downwards as your family situation changes.

Finally, many budgets fail because of excess credit buying and no long-range accumulation to be used as collateral to reduce loan rates or for making future purchases. The wise use of credit is discussed in chapter 4.

Building Your Money Management Plan

Are you ready to begin building your own family budget? Get out your pencil and a notebook with a lot of clean pages, call the family together and complete the following steps. Remember that financial security and enjoyment will not come through pinching pennies but by honestly trying to get a dollar's worth out of each dollar spent. These steps will help you discover the secret of "stretching" your family income to the point of fulfilling your purposes and "buying that dream."

Step 1. Determine Your Goals

The first step in building a money management plan is not the listing of bills, as you might think, but a listing of what you and your family want. You must know this before you can work out the details of a budget.

In determining your goals, plan as though you will live forever. Reach as far into the future as you dare, but be as specific as you can. Also be realistic. Goals will change as the size, age, and income of your family change. It is important for the entire family to be involved in goal-setting. Consider all of the suggestions so that everyone will feel that he has made a contribution. Determine which goals are the most important and give priority to those goals that will benefit the entire family.

Write your goals down according to priority. Some are to be achieved within the year, some in the near future, others from five to twenty years away.

Long-range goals: It will probably be helpful to think of these first. They are the ones you hope to reach in ten or twenty years or perhaps even longer. They may include such things as a college education for the children, your own debt-free home, or a comfortable retirement.

_____   _____

_____   _____

_____   _____

Goals for the next five years: These goals may include such things as the purchase of a new automobile, the down payment on a house, braces for the children's teeth, or an increase in your contributions to the church.

_____   _____

_____   _____

_____   _____

Goals for this year: Your goals for this year may include such things as reducing your installment debts, buying a new washing machine, or beginning music lessons for the children.

_____   _____

_____   _____

_____   _____

After you and your family have decided on your goals, write them down in the notebook so that you can refer to them as you build your own family budget. Your budget should include some savings toward long-term as well as immediate goals so that you will not be tempted to let the goals for this year push your other goals aside.

Step 2. Estimate Your Income

Before you can plan wisely you need to know how much money will be available for the year and by the week. Therefore, the second step in building your budget is to estimate your family income. Most families set up their budgets on a twelve-month period. However, if this is your first attempt to develop a money management plan, you may want to set it up for a three-month period, then review and revise it as necessary to cover the rest of the year. List all regular moneys your family expects to receive during the year: salaries, gifts, and other incomes that are certain. Also list variable income anticipated: Christmas bonus, interest from bonds and savings, dividends from stocks, rents, and other sources. The following guide should be helpful as you list your income in your notebook.

Estimate of Our Total Income
1. Annual wages or income from business (less taxes, social security, and other deductions) .... $_____
2. Interest or dividends from bonds and investments .... _____
3. Income from other family members .... _____
4. Other income .... _____
   Total Annual Income .... _____
   Total Weekly Income (divide annual income by 52).... _____

If your income varies greatly, you should make two estimates. Estimate both the smallest and largest incomes you can reasonably expect. Base your budget on the low-income figure and plan how you will use additional amounts should they become available.

Step 3. Estimate Your Fixed Expenses

Now that you have established your family goals and estimated how much income you will have for the year and by the week, it is time to estimate your fixed expenses. If you have records of family spending, they can serve as the basis for the budget. If these are not available, checkbook stubs, receipts, and old bills will help you estimate these fairly accurately. List each item of expense that your family had along with the amount you spent on each item. These are items over which you have little control. They come due regularly. Your budget will help you save to meet these so that, when they do come due, you will have enough money to pay them. These expenses include such things as rent or mortgage payments, household items such as fuel and electricity, taxes, and installment payments. (Spiraling

inflation will affect such things as fuel and electricity. Allow
for this as you estimate these expenses.) Notice that "church
contributions" and "savings" are both listed as fixed expenses.
The Christian will want to give Christ priority as he develops
his budget. Giving should never be a "leftover after essential
expenditures" item. Savings is the amount you pay yourself for
future needs and wants. Both should be given priority along
with other essentials. The following guide should be helpful as
you list these expenses in your notebook.

Estimate of Our Fixed Expenses

1. Church and other contributions
   Church contributions (annual commitment) .... $_____
   Other contributions or donations .... _____
2. Housing
   Rent or mortgage payments .... _____
   Insurance.. _____
   Taxes .... _____
   Fuel .... _____
   Water... _____
   Electricity .... _____
   Phone... _____
   Other items.. _____
3. Debts and obligations
   Total installment payments (itemize on separate
      page)... _____
   Other debts.. _____
4. Insurance
   Life .... _____
   Health .... _____
   Auto.. _____
   Other .... _____
5. Taxes, fees, and licenses
   Taxes (list those not included elsewhere).................... _____
   Professional fees or union dues .... _____
   Licenses (auto, drivers, pets, etc.)................................ _____
6. Savings .... _____

7. Other items

_____ .... _____

_____ .... _____

_____ .... _____

Total Annual Fixed Expenses.. _____

Total Weekly Fixed Expenses (divide annual expenses
by 52) .... _____

Add the fixed expenses and divide the total by 52. This will be the amount you will need to spend or set aside each week in order to have the necessary amount of money when the bills come due. You may find it necessary to place this in a special checking or savings account or other place where you will not be tempted to spend it on other items. It is absolutely necessary that this amount be held in reserve in order to meet the fixed expenses.

List these in your notebook with the date that each will come due. In this way you can plan ahead so that you will have the amount available at the appropriate time.

Step 4. Set Up an Emergency Fund

One of the most important steps in building your budget is to provide an emergency fund. There are always those times in every family when things go wrong or emergencies occur. It is said that the average family is one that has an unexpected expense every month—but doesn't expect to have one this month! Perhaps an unexpected medical bill develops, the refrigerator plays out, or the fuel pump on the car stops pumping. When this happens, the only thing that can be done is to dip into the emergency fund. By setting something aside every week into your emergency fund, you will be able to meet these unexpected bills without wrecking your entire budget. Most people agree that with proper insurance to take care of crisis situations, your

emergency fund should equal two or three months' income.
When your emergency fund reaches this amount, put the extra
money into regular savings, in investments to help your family
realize its goals, or into something else your family needs or
wants.

Our Emergency Fund
1. Put aside each week for emergencies .... $_____
2. We will let this fund accumulate until it reaches
   three months' salary .... Total $_____

Step 5. Estimate Your Flexible Expenses

Your flexible expenses are those over which you might have
the most control. Although they are regular in time, they vary
in amounts. How you divide these expenses into different categories is up to you. They include such things as the necessary
money to run the house, transportation, school lunches and other
expenses, ordinary doctor bills, and recreation. Include in these
amounts something for each member of the family in the way
of an allowance to be used just as the individual desires. This
will help to keep the budget from becoming a distasteful chore.
Family members should not have to account for how this amount
is used. It is for personal wants and desires. Here again it is
vital to consider inflation. The amount budgeted for an area
may be adequate in January but may not be sufficient by Oc-
tober. Consider each area carefully.

The following guide should be helpful as you list your flexible
expenses in your notebook.

Estimate of Our Flexible Expenses
1. Food .... $_____
2. Household supplies .... _____
3. Home improvements, furnishings,
   and maintenance .... _____
4. Cleaning and laundry .... _____
5. Transportation (include car operation and minor

repairs) .... _____
6. Clothing .... _____
7. Medical and dental bills .... _____
8. Drug bills .... _____
9. School, lunches and supplies... _____
10. Lunches (for working members of the family) .... _____
11. Subscriptions .... _____
12. Recreation.. _____
13. Gifts (Christmas, birthday, wedding, etc.) .... _____
14. Personal allowances—Father .... $_____
                      Mother .... _____
                      Others .... _____
                      Total .... $_____
15. Vacation (set something aside each week) .... $_____
16. Other items and miscellaneous.................................... _____
    Total Annual Flexible Expenses.................................... _____
    Total Weekly Flexible Expenses (divide annual
    expenses by 52) .... $_____

Total the amount you and your family have estimated for your flexible expenses and divide the total by 52. This will be the amount you will plan to spend, or set aside, each week to cover these items.

Step 6. Compare Income and Expenses

This is where you will actually begin to see what your financial picture looks like. Take your weekly income and subtract your allowance for fixed expenses and your emergency fund. This is the amount you have left each week to pay all your day-to-day expenses. To know whether or not your budget will work, you must compare this figure to the total for flexible expenses. The following guide should be helpful as you figure this in your notebook.

Our Balance Sheet
1. Our weekly income is... $_____
2. Our fixed expenses are (subtract from weekly

    income) .... _____

           Amount left .... _____

3. Our emergency fund is (subtract from above
    total) .... _____

           Amount left .... _____

4. Our flexible expenses are (subtract from above
    total) .... _____

           This is what is left after all expenses .... $_____

How did you do? Ideally, you will have some money left over after all expenses have been taken care of. If so, you can either increase some of the items or put the amount in savings for the future. If the total for flexible expenses is larger than the amount available, you will have to go back and reduce the allotment for some of the items.

Remember to keep your plan flexible. Your budget must be able to stretch with your needs. One month you may need to stretch at one point where the need is greater and, at the same time, cut down at another point. The plan must fit *your* family. No two families spend their incomes in exactly the same way or put priorities on the same things.

When you and your family have agreed on goals and have developed an agreed upon money management plan to help these "dreams" come true, it will be necessary to keep some records of your spending habits. You will find it easier to keep track of these if you will use a family financial record book. This does not need to be elaborate or expensive. You may either use the notebook that you have started with, or you can find several types of financial record books in variety and stationery stores. Also many banks, credit unions, and insurance companies will provide such record books free of charge. Be careful not to make your bookkeeping too detailed or too demanding or you may give it up without a fair try. You may need to keep a week-by-week record for awhile to determine just where your money is going. However, you should soon find that a monthly budget will fit your needs best if it is properly planned. The important thing is to keep your total expenditures in approximate balance with income.

There are books written about family budgeting. There are even more books written about dieting—and the analogy is apt. Don't most of us really know how we can lose weight? By cutting down on our eating, especially of certain foods. The same is true of making a family budget work. If you have trouble making ends meet, you know—or you had better find out—where you can cut down on your spending. It's as simple as that.[3]

For Your Consideration

1. *What do surveys indicate about money and family problems?*
2. *Why is good money management an imperative for the Christian family?*
3. *What is the real purpose of a budget?*
4. *Why is it important to tailor a budget to fit your own family's living needs and wishes?*
5. *Do you feel that it is important to include the entire family in money management decisions? Why?*
6. *What are the three basic reasons why families get into financial difficulty?*
7. *Review the six suggested steps for developing your own family budget.*

Notes

1. United Buying Service Consumer's Handbook, The Benjamin Company, Inc., 485 Madison Avenue, New York, New York 10022, 1973.

2. "Dollarwise"—The Dreyfus Family Money Management Newsletter #15.

3. *How Much Are You Worth?* The Dreyfus Family Money Management Service, 225 Park Avenue, South, New York, N. Y. 10003, 1974, p. 32.

4.
GETTING
IN AND
OUT OF DEBT
(Taking Care of Unpaid Bills!)

Almost every family experiences a lack of funds at some time. The preceding chapter on "Why and How to Build a Budget" suggested steps to set up a wise money management plan that should help families avoid such a situation. But suppose that you suddenly find yourself in a financial crisis. Perhaps you don't yet have an emergency fund sufficient to meet the crisis. It may be that you become sick and can't work and your income is drastically reduced. Or, you may have given in to the lure of easy credit and overextended yourself to the point where you cannot make your payments. On the other hand, your situation may be like that of the family talking to the financial counselor. You want to know the answer to the same question they were asking, "How can we get out of debt?" The answer may not be easy, but it's there if you will look for it. An equally important question that should be answered is "How did we get so deeply in debt in the first place?" Let's answer that question first, in the hope that an understanding of the "why" will help many people avoid the necessity of asking "how?"

Causes of Extreme Indebtedness

We have already noted the three basic reasons why families get into financial difficulty, but let's review them briefly.

1. *Failure to set anything aside for an emergency fund.* Setting

aside an emergency fund is "easier said than done." All of us are tempted to budget all available income without allowing anything for an emergency. We hope to get by without an emergency until expenses are lighter. But an emergency may strike at any time, so it is vital to be prepared.

2. *Budgeting more than the net take-home pay.* Remember that the amount deducted for taxes, retirement, hospitalization, and other such items cannot be considered as available income. You can only spend your *net* take-home pay, and if you budget more than that amount you will soon find yourself in a financial crisis.

3. *Overextended credit buying.* Credit can be good, but if it is overextended it can create a real financial burden. When credit is too easy to obtain, persons sometimes lack the discipline to use it wisely and therefore incur so many debts that the payments cannot be met. Christians have a definite responsibility to meet their bills. Some Christians, even some ministers, have lost an effective witness in their communities because of their inability to meet their financial obligations. This makes it imperative for you to avoid overextended credit buying.

Each of the above is the result of a lack of education in the money management area. Unfortunately, most people have never had any kind of training in the wise use of money. As a result, most families learn only from experience and many find themselves so deeply in debt that they must seek professional help.

Extreme indebtedness may also be the result of some additional causes. Look at some of the possibilities. First, consider your flexible expenses. Are your food bills constantly over the amount allotted? Do you purchase the best of everything, including the most expensive cuts of meat, fresh vegetables out of season, and frozen convenience items? If your clothing expenses are too high, you may find the answer in your clothes closet. Some people have a compulsion to buy clothes. Even if it was on sale, it was no bargain if you didn't really need it. How about those utility bills? You can save some extra money with just a little effort by turning lights off when not in use or closing the door and turning down the heat in a room that is seldom used. Look each item over carefully. When the record of what you are spending indicates that something is higher than you think it should be, it is time to examine it carefully.

Now take a look at your fixed expenses. They may be causing part of the problem. Are you paying more than you should for rent or the purchase of a home? Most family budget counselors generally agree that the figure should be between 15 and 25 percent of your net income. Some people deliberately choose expensive neighborhoods simply for status and prestige. How about your automobiles? Do you really need two? Could you reduce your indebtedness and get along just as well with one? Or if you have only one, could it be a less expensive model and still provide adequate transportation? If transportation costs are excessive, it could be because you live a long way from your work. Perhaps you could move closer, and cut both housing and transportation costs. On the other hand, it might mean that you couldn't have a garden and your food costs would go up.

Any one of these could be the cause of your trouble or the cause of trouble in the future. Maybe it is something else. A close examination can provide the answer to current problems as well as help to prevent problems in the future.

Indebtedness is not a new problem, although it has been intensified by inflation and the demands of modern living. For example, most young couples want to begin their married lives with all of the conveniences that their parents have. They do not stop to realize that their parents have worked most of their lifetime to accumulate their possessions. Neither is a financial crisis a respecter of people or positions. The man in debt may be your best friend or closest relative. He may be the best foreman in his plant or the lowest paid on the staff. People from every walk of life and in all income brackets get into debt. Remember that it is not the amount of money, but how we manage what we have that counts.

Suggestions for Solving the Problem

Before you look at the suggested steps for getting out of debt, consider carefully two things that you should *avoid.*

1. Don't borrow money just to try to keep your friends and neighbors from finding out that you are in debt. It's true that you are under a great deal of pressure. You are carrying a heavy load on your shoulders, and you have a distracting worry on your mind. But it is better to deal with the problem honestly and openly than to complicate the situation through a temporary solution.

2. Never run away from your debts. There is no way a Christian can justify his failure to honestly face up to his obligations. If you try to run away, you will lose your self-respect as well as the respect of others. More and more people recognize the misfortune of getting into debt as simply a lack of skill in money management. There is no disgrace in debt, but there is in failure to try to honestly meet your obligations.

Probably the best advice that can be given to anyone in a financial crisis is to seek professional help if possible. The chances are that your local United Fund or Community Chest office can advise you about where to get professional money management counseling at low fees, or in some instances at no fee at all. Many times credit unions, labor unions, banks, savings and loan associations, and similar institutions have money management experts willing to give advice to families in a financial crisis. If you live in a rural or suburban area, your county extension agent may be able to offer advice or suggest a source of help.

If you wish to try to solve your problems yourself, the following steps are suggested to help you get out of your financial crisis.

Step 1. Begin with a Family Conference

Just as it is important for family members to agree on building a budget, it is equally important for family members to be included in developing a plan to maintain family needs, while at the same time making progress toward freedom from overindebtedness. At first you may have feelings of defeat and embarrassment. These feelings will be short-lived if you will put your family's mental efforts to work to solve the problem rather than worry about it fruitlessly.

Step 2. List Your Past Unpaid Bills

Use the "Our Debt Payment Plan" chart provided at the end of this chapter as a guide. Draw up your own plan in the notebook you have been using to keep track of your financial affairs. List the name of the company, bank, or whomever you owe and the address. Then list the name of some person you can contact about the debt and his phone number. Next list the total amount due on each account along with the total of all debts. The family should be able to help you be sure that you haven't overlooked bills which could come up later and ruin your entire plan. Getting out of debt is important to the entire family and must have the enthusiastic support of all members.

Now consider each item and list the amount of the present monthly payment and the date it is due. Since most bills of this nature come due monthly, it will be easier to figure on this basis. If a bill is due weekly or quarterly, figure the monthly amount and enter that amount in this column. After you have filled in this information on each item, add the figures to determine the amount due on all bills each month.

Step 3. Analyze Your Current Budget

This step involves using the figure you developed for your family money management plan in the preceding chapter. Is there anything in the "emergency fund" or anything left in the last blank after all expenses were subtracted from your weekly income? Probably not if you are already in a financial crisis. If so, this amount may be applied against your debts.

Now it will be important for the family to reexamine the entire budget. Go over each expense. Discuss it with the family and decide how important it is in relation to cutting back in order to get out of debt. Your flexible expenses offer the best possibility for finding the necessary funds. You may have to cut out some new clothes, economize on food, and drastically reduce allotments for gifts, vacation, allowances, and other areas that can be cut.

In addition to cutting living expenses, another possibility is to search for hidden assets which might be used to provide additional funds for debt repayment. One example might be the cash value of life insurance policies. Sometimes a loan can be obtained against a policy, but it should be remembered that your protection is reduced until this amount is repaid. It should be considered only in an extreme emergency. Consult your insurance agent for more information.

It might also be wise to consider obtaining a consolidation loan from your bank or credit union. Under this arrangement, you get a new loan from one lender to pay off other debts. This means that you will have one large debt instead of several smaller ones. It also means that total monthly payments will be smaller in most cases, since the repayment period is usually longer. Use extreme caution in considering this. Consolidation loans often carry a high rate of interest and sometimes include other objectionable features. Unless you investigate carefully and understand exactly what is required, you could end up in worse financial shape than you are already in.

There are two figures which you must get into proper alignment—the amount you have left from your income after fixed and flexible expenses, and the amount which you owe your creditors. This will require some real sacrifice on the part of each family member, but it will be worth it. When you have finished your analysis, you will come up with the maximum amount you can use each week to reduce your bills. Since your family budget was developed on a weekly basis, you will need to multiply this amount by 4.33 to find out how much you will have each month. (This is due to the fact that there are 13 weeks in each quarter. This is equal to four and one-third weeks each month.) For example, you may find that you will have $12.50 per week to apply to your debts. Multiply this by 4.33 as follows:

$$\begin{array}{r} \$12.50 \quad \text{(weekly amount)} \\ \underline{4.33} \quad \text{(weeks in a month)} \\ 3750 \\ 3750 \\ \underline{5000} \\ 541250 \quad \text{or } \$54.12 \text{ monthly} \end{array}$$

Step 4. Determine Payment to Each Creditor

This step is one of the most difficult you will have. Determine how much of the money you have available for monthly debt payments should be sent to each creditor. It will be necessary to consider many things as you try to get the best possible results from every available dollar. First, look carefully at the list of debts. See if there are any items that could be returned for credit or sold for enough to pay off the balance. You may find some items that are worth no more than you owe on them, and the family would not encounter any hardship without them.

Using your "Our Debt Payment Plan" chart, divide the monthly amount and write down by each creditor the amount that you think will be fair to pay him. Some of your bills will require a larger monthly payment than others. This should be determined in relation to the balance due. Also consider what will give you the best advantage. It may be possible to pay off some small items relatively soon and then that amount can be added to the amount paid other creditors. Now write down the date that each creditor will be paid in full.

Step 5. Present Your New Payment Plan

When you have done this, you will have a completely new plan to present to the people you owe. No matter how much the debt or the amount of the payment, this will represent an honest effort to meet your obligations. Now talk personally with each creditor, show him your plan, and ask for his agreement. Most creditors will respect your efforts and cooperate with your new plan. In most cases it may mean paying additional interest charges or other fees. One word of caution, do not assume that the bill is automatically eliminated on an item you are buying on credit, such as a car, when that item is repossessed. The price that the repossessed item brings at a forced sale may not cover the entire amount of the debt you owe after repossession costs are added on. You could end up without the item, and still owe money on it.

In rare cases, some creditor may not agree with your new plan and threaten to take action against you unless you pay him more than his fair share of your earnings. If this happens, you can remind him that other creditors are in a position to take the same action. This would mean that everyone would lose. After all, you are making an honest effort to meet your obligations; and you and your family are the ones that will have to sacrifice in order to get out of debt.

When you have started this plan, stick with it! It will take a great deal of determination, but it will be worth it. Make your payments promptly. If something should come up to prevent your making a payment on time, be sure to notify every creditor affected. You asked for his cooperation, and it is only fair to keep him posted on your progress or lack of it. Also be certain that the money designated for debt payment is set aside for that purpose and not used for anything else!

When your family develops and successfully completes a plan to overcome a serious financial crisis, they will have mastered some of the most difficult and most important areas of money management. Just as soon as you begin to clear up your debts, put these abilities to work to plan for the kind of life you wanted before you ran into debt. You have learned from experience that you can plan for something really worthwhile and make it come about.

For Your Consideration

1. *Review the three basic reasons why families get into financial difficulty.*

2. *What are some of the additional causes for extreme indebtedness?*

3. *Name the two things you should avoid doing if you find yourself in a critical financial difficulty.*

4. *What is the* best *advice you can give to anyone in a financial crisis?*

5. *List the five suggested steps for getting out of debt.*

6. *What can you do if some creditor does not agree with your plan and threatens to take action against you?*

7. *How can you put the valuable lessons you have learned from experience into a plan for something really worthwhile?*

Our Debt Payment Plan

Monthly amount available for debt payment $ _____ *

	CREDITOR Name–Address	Contact Person Name–Phone Number	Amount Owed	Present Payment	Date Due	New Payment	Paid in Full Date!
1							
2							
3							
4							
5							
6							
	Monthly Totals		$	$		$ *	

*These two totals should be the same.

5.
SPENDING WITH A PURPOSE

(In the Image of God)

"Then God said, 'Let us make a man—someone like ourselves, to be master of all life upon the earth and in the skies and in the seas.' So God made man like his Maker. Like God did God make man; Man and maid did he make them. And God blessed them and told them, 'Multiply and fill the earth and subdue it; you are masters of the fish and birds and all the animals' " (Gen. 1:26-28 TLB).

God chose man for a very special place in the world. Man was the climax of God's good creation. He is a part of the created order and shares many things in common with the rest of creation. But man is different! He is set apart from the rest of creation by the very choice of God. He is different because he is made "in the image of God." This difference is given only to man.

In his book *Living the Responsible Life*, Cecil Ray says: "Man's responsibility is to 'image'—that is, to reflect God. . . . That is, man's life, attitudes, and actions are to reflect God and his purpose in action. . . . Man is to go around 'imaging God.' He is to mirror God's love, character, and purpose. What God is like, man is to demonstrate in action. What God wants done— man is to perform." [1]

Not only did God make man in his image, he also gave him the authority and responsibility to control the rest of the material world. This responsibility carries with it the understanding that man will exercise this authority under God, to achieve God's purposes.

The Christian will strive to "image God" in all of life. He will seek to be responsible for all he possesses. This becomes his life-style. He will reflect God's control in his life, not only as he attempts to build a budget, but as he seriously considers the purpose of all of his spending. He will consider his own needs in the light of the needs of the world. He will often ask, "Will this purchase reflect Christ's control in my life? Will it help fulfill God's purpose in his material world?"

Important Principles of Spending

There comes a time in money management when you stop planning and start buying. A knowledge of how to spend your money is just as important as how to build a budget. On paper your budget may look pretty good; but unless you know how to spend the dollars that have been allocated for each area, the plan may be of very little value. This chapter will cover some of the basic areas of spending. But first let's look at some principles that apply to buying almost anything.

Decide *what* to buy. In any transaction, there is a buyer and a seller. The seller makes a living by convincing you to buy his product. He is trained and committed to that purpose, else he would not be in business. The key issue here is whether you are being "sold" a product or services, or whether you are "buying." (You can be either the "hunter" or the "hunted.") Too many shoppers allow themselves to be "sold" rather than using their own initiative, intelligence, and independence.[2] Many merchants estimate that as much as 70 percent of their goods are bought on impulse.

All your spending should be done in light of the objectives and goals which your family has set for itself. No matter what your income is, it must be made to cover all your wants and needs. If you spend too much in one area, something else must suffer. The conscientious Christian will try to keep all of these elements in balance.

Don't buy more than you want or *need*. Before you go on a shopping spree, it is important to know what you want and need and limit your spending to those things. For example, if you are buying a new washing machine, you should decide in general terms what you need that machine to do. Every extra gadget and button will increase the price. The special "mini-basket" might be nice—if you will really use it enough to warrant the extra cost. An automobile battery with a five-year guarantee selling for $36.95 is probably a better buy than a battery with a two-year guarantee selling for $22.95—*if* you plan to keep the car more than two years.

Determine the *quality* of what you are buying. Few of us can afford to always buy the best brands of everything—but neither can we afford to buy cheap merchandise that will not last as long as we need it. It is always good to shop around for major purchases, including food, to find the best quality at the price you can afford.

It is good to both "beware" of and "be aware" of sales. Some companies use the old "bait and switch" method in advertising. They advertise an item at an extremely low price to get you into the store—then they try to switch your attention to a "much better" (and much more expensive) item. Items on "sale" can provide a good savings if you really need them and if they are from the regular stock. "Special purchase" items are merchandise bought for a particular sale and may not be worth even the cost of the special sale price. Beware of the special gimmicks and the company that is always having a "going out of business" sale. Be aware of actual sales of reputable dealers where you may find something you really need at an extremely good price.

The salesman explained that the new home freezer would pay for itself with savings on food bills. But the housewife answered, "Yes, but we're already buying our car on the bus fares we save, our washing machine on the laundry bills we save, and our house on the rent we save. We just can't afford to save any more right now." [3]

Another important factor is knowing *when* to buy. This is one of the most important ways to get the most for your dollar. This involves planning ahead in two areas: (1) budget planning so that the money will be available; (2) need planning so that you will know the best time to buy what you really need. Mary knows that the family needs some new towels and washcloths. She also knows that the "white sales" are in January and that if she will keep some of the money in the household budget until then she can get a better buy for her money. However, knowing when to buy may not always be aimed at getting more for your dollar. Your goal may be to get the best selections before the merchandise is picked-over by everyone else. Then you need to know when the market stocks fresh produce and bakery goods and that spring styles start arriving in the stores in February and fall styles in August.

A final word of general advice is to know *where* to buy. It is always wise to buy from reputable dealers. These dealers will stand behind their products. Your satisfaction will be their primary concern. Their prices are normally no higher than the "bargain barn" and the quality may be far superior. Avoid dealers that will not accept merchandise that you may find unsatisfactory and want to return. Also avoid those who insist that items are guaranteed by the "manufacturer" that produced them and don't stand behind a guarantee themselves. It may be difficult for you to get in touch with the manufacturer and work out a satisfactory settlement. Reputable dealers are an asset to your community; they deserve your patronage, and they will serve you well. If you have doubts about a dealer, call your Better Business Bureau for advice.

Now let's give our attention to some of the major areas of spending.

Your Food Dollar

How many times have you gone into the supermarket determined not to spend more than $40 for your groceries, only to come out after spending $55? Most families in America spend between 20 and 25 percent of their income for food. There are ways to buy all the nutritional food your family needs and spend less. The secret is *planning*.

Plan where to buy. Become familiar with all the stores in your area and know what advantage each has. Some may be consistently lower on some items than others. Some may run specials on a few items to lure you in, but may be higher on other essentials.

Plan what to buy. This is one of the best ways to save money on food. Know what your family likes and needs. Look at the weekly ads in your newspaper to determine any special buys on these items. You may even plan your meals for the week around these special buys. Then make a shopping list and stick to it! A list will help you fight off impulse buying. Fresh fruits and vegetables are your best buy when they are in season. Use them freely. Avoid them when they are out of season and the price is high.

As you plan what to buy, determine the quantities you can use. The "large economy size" is usually a good buy, *if* you use it all. If half of it goes to waste you have lost money. You may be able to buy in larger quantities and store some if you have a home freezer. You may also be able to purchase meats during a special sale or buy the side or quarter at a reduced price and save money. You can also save a substantial amount, and often improve the quality, by canning or freezing fruits and vegetables in season.

Be aware of the extra cost of "instant," precooked, and frozen foods. They are only a good buy when the convenience or quality is really worth the extra price. Quality is always a consideration in food buying. The cheapest brand is not necessarily the best buy. Become familiar with the various grades, brands, and standards. Don't let the package fool you—it's the contents you're interested in.

Know when to shop. Many stores offer their specials on the weekend. Sometimes you can pick up a real bargain at the produce counter on Saturday evening. Produce that may not keep over the weekend may be something you can use right now and it may be marked down for a quick sale. Above all, don't shop when you are hungry! Everything will look good and you'll spend much more. A sandwich or milkshake is a good investment if you haven't eaten recently.

Your Clothing Dollar

An adequate wardrobe for each member of the family doesn't depend on how much money you spend. It depends on careful planning and management of your clothing dollars. When you buy clothes there are some major points to consider to be sure that you get your money's worth.

1. *What do you need?* Make an inventory of what you already have. Then you can determine what you really need. You can get variety through changing accessories. Stick to basic styles that will not quickly date your wardrobe. If you must buy "fads," limit them to a few inexpensive items.

Provide for your immediate needs first. Then you can begin your long-range buying that can really save money. If your inventory shows that Dad is short on dress shirts and your daughter will soon need a new coat, determine when these can be purchased at the best price. The items that you "have to have right now" usually cost the most. Try to buy those items that you need regularly when they are on sale. Wise planning for future needs can save many dollars.

2. *Where should you buy?* It is always important to compare values and prices. Prices may vary in different stores even on identical items. This may be determined by the location of the store and its operating costs. An item of equal quality at a lower price is a good buy regardless of where you get it.

Buy from stores that are known for their quality. These are the stores that will stand behind their sales. Also, know what services a store offers. Some stores will alter a garment that you purchase from them for the life of the garment. If Dad goes on a diet and loses weight and the pants of a suit have to be taken up, free alterations can save you some money.

Many manufacturers have outlet stores in or near their plants. If you travel, or live near these, they usually offer exceptional buys. One man who travels through North Carolina annually buys all of his families' socks and hose from an outlet store of a major manufacturer at a substantial savings.

Don't overlook the bargain basement of major department stores. They sometimes have exceptional values. Sometimes these may be items that are slightly "irregulars," or items that didn't sell quickly in regular stock. If they have items you need, they may be a good buy.

3. *When should you buy?* It has become standard practice for stores to run clearance sales at certain times of the year. Take advantage of these when they can meet your needs. If you know that you are going to need a new dress or suit next fall, you can save by buying it when it is on sale in the spring. Or why buy a pair of shoes now when you know they will be on sale in a few weeks? The selection may not be as good, but the value for the dollars you spend will be much better.

On the other hand, don't develop "bargainitis." Make sure that the clothes you buy meet your needs. It's no bargain if you don't need it and use it after you buy it.

4. *What should you buy?* Fabric, workmanship, fit, and style are all important considerations related to what you should buy. You usually get the best value for your dollar when you buy the finest quality you can afford. This may be the middle-price lines. You may not need the hand-tailoring of a more expensive suit or dress. Be certain that the fabric is of a good quality, that the item fits properly, and that the style is not only current but will last.

When buying for your children, remember that it is probably not a good idea to buy an expensive suit or dress if you know that he will outgrow it before he gets full value from it. Look for ample seams, deep hems or cuffs, and other features that might make alterations possible as the child grows.

It is always better to have a few quality pieces of clothing that will last and retain their original beauty than to have a lot of cheap clothes that don't look good after just a few wearings. Smart sales shopping, combined with good long-range planning, can help you get by with fewer and often better clothes at a lower cost.

Your Housing Dollar

At least once in your lifetime you'll have to make the decision of whether it is best for you to rent or buy a house. This may be the most important financial decision you will ever make. If you decide to buy, it will probably be the largest single investment you'll ever make. Before you make this decision you should analyze your personal desires, the permanence of your work, your income, your savings, the size of your family, and how handy you are at repairing and maintaining a house. Entire books have been written on housing, so we can only consider the most basic fundamentals here.

Renting may be the best answer for you if:

You are single and live alone.

You are a young married couple with limited income.

Your work requires you to be away a great deal and you like the security of not worrying about home while you are away.

Your work involves periodic transfers.

You are retired, the children are gone, and you enjoy the lighter responsibilities of maintenance.

When you rent, your situation is more flexible and adaptable to change. You may enjoy the added benefits of a swimming pool, tennis courts, and golf club. You do not reduce your cash savings for a down payment on a house. You do not have to worry about a mortgage, property taxes, mowing the lawn, painting, plumbing, and other maintenance problems.

Buying a home may be the best answer if:

You enjoy the sense of independence, stability, and security that comes from owning.

You can afford the down payment without completely depleting your ready reserve.

You prefer a home for rearing your children.

Your present work is relatively permanent.

You are able, either personally or financially, to provide the necessary maintenance.

If you decide to buy a house, one of the first questions you will have to answer is, "What price house can we afford?" Some authorities maintain that the cost of a house should not exceed two-and-a-half times your gross annual income. The company that holds the mortgage will also have something to say about this, as you will have to "qualify" for a loan. That means that they will determine if your income is sufficient to cover the monthly payment. You may want to check with your bank, a realtor, or a mortgage company first to see how much financial load your income will bear.

A second question you will need to answer is, "Where should we buy?" The Christian should give special attention to this answer. A house in the "best" part of town will cost more than the same house in a "good" part of town. How important is the status that comes from living in the best part of town? Of course, there will be other considerations: Are the schools adequate for the children? Is it close enough to work and shopping that extra time and expense will not be wasted in travel? Is the house priced according to comparable homes in the neighborhood? Will it meet all your family needs? Can you live here comfortably without living above your means?

Another important question is, "What kind of house should we buy?" If you expect your family to grow, you may not be able to buy the house you will ultimately need. However, you can look for a house with expansion possibilities. Or, you can look for a house that would have a good resale value if you decide to sell and move to a larger house later. Keep in mind sound construction and maintenance needs. A frame house will require the added cost of frequent painting. A brick or stone house may cost more initially but might be the best buy in the long run.

"How shall we finance our house?" will also have to be answered. Putting down as much cash as you can and holding your interest charges to a minimum may not be the best answer for you. If you are thinking of resale at a future date, a small amount down and a high mortgage (at the lowest possible rate) can be an advantage. A buyer doesn't have to have as much cash to assume your loan if you have a relatively small equity in your house.

When you have a large mortgage, you are paying a large amount of interest on your loan. However, the interest is a tax deduction which reduces the actual cost. You may find a better way to invest your extra funds than placing them all in a house. Inflation can also reduce the cost of a loan. In 1967 a 6¼ percent loan looked pretty steep; but by 1974 when interest rates on home loans had risen to 8½ percent, the 6¼ percent looked extremely good.

There are also good reasons for making a large down payment and having a relatively small mortgage. Your monthly payments will be smaller or you can finance the mortgage over a shorter period of time, thus saving substantially on interest. A large equity in your home will help protect you against unexpected financial emergencies. The mortgage company will be more willing to help you through a crisis when they know that you have a substantial amount in your house. You may also be able to obtain a mortgage loan against your equity.

Wherever you live and whatever kind of house you decide to buy, protect it by keeping it constantly in good condition to prevent deterioration and to avoid major repairs. Protect your house with adequate insurance. Protect your family with adequate insurance to pay off the debt if anything should happen to you.

Your Transportation Dollar

Next to food, clothing, and housing, the most expensive item for many families is transportation. This is especially true if you own a new car or more than one car and are making payments on them. This is another area that the Christian will want to consider carefully. It is easy to "need" two cars when all your friends and neighbors have two. On the other hand, you might really need two cars, even if the neighbors only have one. Your own needs and your family goals will determine the right decision for you.

Know how much it costs you to operate and maintain your

car for a year. Also consider how you use your car. If you are on the road a great deal, you may need the safety and comfort of a larger automobile. If you primarily drive a few miles to work and back each day, a compact may fit your needs just as well. A recent survey indicated that including depreciation, maintenance, fuel, etc., it costs 24 cents a mile to operate a standard size car for a year. Proper maintenance and good driving habits can help hold your car operating costs to a minimum.

Many people ask when they should trade in their car. Unfortunately, there is no easy answer to this question. It depends on the car and its owner. A Transportation Department study, by E. M. Cope and C. L. Gauthier, noted:

> Assuming a normal amount of driving, keeping a car after it is two years old does save some money, but not very much. Therefore, except in states where there is a substantial property tax on the value of the car, and for financing charges, any decision to trade a car or keep it a while longer should be based on the owner's tastes and circumstances, rather than on any thought of increasing or decreasing his cents-per-mile of owning and operating costs. As far as economy is concerned, he can make the decision with a clear conscience.[1]

When you decide to buy a new car, decide what you want and need before visiting the dealers' showrooms. Impulse buying is a great threat when it comes to automobile buying. Remember, too, that it pays to shop around. You may save several hundred dollars by comparing prices. Get the best possible price on the new car and for the old one you are trading in. You can probably get a better deal if you sell your old car yourself and buy the new one without a trade-in.

Prices are always highest when the new models first come out. Prices usually drop significantly in December and drastically in the summer before new models arrive. If you plan to keep a car for several years, you may want to take advantage of the price cut in the summer. However, you should know that just as soon as the new models arrive the depreciation on your car will be the same as on one bought eight months earlier. Your car will be a "year old" no matter when you bought it.

Your Recreation and Leisure Dollar

Too often, in our concentration on food, clothing, housing, and other necessities, we overlook the importance of the families' recreation and leisure needs. Most budget experts say that every family should allocate some money for "fun." This may include recreation, hobbies, vacation, and other forms of entertainment. Your family needs a change of pace from time to time. If funds are limited, you should become familiar with community facilities and activities that can provide free or relatively inexpensive recreation. This might include museums, libraries, parks, amateur sporting events, and concerts.

If entertainment and recreation mean more to you than acquiring something more lasting, face up to the fact and make it part of your budget planning. Just as in other areas, every family has different needs and desires and the way you spend your money should reflect your own family. Even in recreation and leisure, tastes vary. One family may enjoy camping out while another may not. A lady recently said, "My idea of 'roughing it' is doing without a salad fork!" This lady would probably rather spend her vacation money for one week of travel staying in motels, than spend the same amount for three weeks of travel while camping out. Each family must decide for itself, then make the most from every available recreation and leisure dollar.

Adult Toys

One final word concerning your spending. Adults can get hooked on toys just as much as children. Like children, life can become little more than an endless series of wanting and playing with toys. Adult toys cost more.[5]

Adult toys can be almost anything. The list may include your home, clothes, car, electronics, motor bikes, boats, and weekend homes. Actually, there is nothing wrong with any one of these items and in many instances their purchase and use is properly related to the responsible pursuit of the Christian's life.[6] The important thing is to know the difference between your actual needs and your desire for toys. Only by knowing the difference can the Christian "image" God and help meet the needs of the world. Answering the following questions before making any purchase will help you spend with a purpose: "What will this thing do for my life? Will it help me move toward my Christian goals in life? Will it enrich my life and give me a true sense of commitment?"[7]

For Your Consideration

1. What does it mean for the Christian to "image" God?

2. List the general principles that apply to buying almost anything.

3. What are some ways that you can cut down on the high cost of food?

4. Name the four major points to consider when buying clothes.

5. What conditions might make renting more appealing than buying a home?

6. What might be considered unchristian about owning cars?

7. Why should the Christian beware of "adult toys"?

Notes

1. Cecil Ray, *Living the Responsible Life* (Nashville: Convention Press), pp. 8-9 from manuscript.

2. Robert J. Hastings, *How to Manage Your Money* (Nashville: Broadman Press, 1965), p. 47.

3. *Ibid.*, p. 50.

4. A U.S. Department of Transportation study by E. M. Cope and C. L. Gauthier.

5. *Living the Responsible Life*, Ray, p. 86.

6. *Ibid.*, p. 87.

7. *Ibid.*, p. 87.

6.
USE
YOUR CREDIT
WISELY

(Beware of the "Easy-payment!")

The Martins and the Lloyds live next door to each other, but they are miles apart in their use of credit. The early married life of Barbara and Joe Martin was spent during the depression years. They still remember those difficult days. As a result their philosophy is to "stay out of debt." They refuse to borrow money from any source, have no charge accounts, use no credit cards, drive a car for years, buy everything they can on sale, and have an emergency fund equal to six months' salary, in addition to other savings and investments.

Their neighbors, Thelma and Brad Lloyd, were married in 1954 and have never known anything other than the affluent post-World War II American way of life. Their home was purchased on a 100 percent GI loan. They own two automobiles and trade them in nearly every year. They have charge accounts at several local department stores and use credit cards for everything from travel to entertainment. Thelma and Brad both have good jobs. They carry very little cash and don't feel that they need to. If it were not for credit, they would not be enjoying any of their major material belongings. Their philosophy of credit is, "We couldn't live without it!"

Our Credit-Using Society

These lives illustrate the phenomenal changes which have

transformed our society from a cash-paying to a credit-using one. The fact is that ours has become a credit economy. Almost all of us use credit at one time or another, and most of us use it wisely. Only fifty years ago most people condemned installment buying and considered debt a "sin." Now days, virtually every home is purchased with the aid of a mortgage. Two thirds of all new cars are bought on credit. More than a third of all furniture and appliances, such as refrigerators, washing machines, ranges, and television sets are bought on credit. At least half of all American families make installment payments not counting home mortgages.[1] If it were not for credit, many young people would not be able to finish college or other training.

There are advantages to buying with cash which should be noted. First, you cannot spend more than you have. Some unexpected emergency, such as the loss of a job or prolonged illness, will not catch you with a lot of bills you cannot pay. Then, you can buy wherever you find the best price rather than only in the stores where you have charge accounts. Also, some stores will still give you a discount of 3 percent, maybe even 5 percent, if you offer to pay cash. Don't hesitate to ask—you have nothing to lose and much to gain.

Credit today is just a signature away at thousands of places across the country. You are constantly being swamped by attractive appeals to get and use yet another credit card or begin a charge account. The sales clerks in many stores ask, "May I charge this for you?" This in itself should indicate that the store expects to make money on its "easy payment plan." Recent studies show that the average family spends about 18 percent of its after-tax income in installment payments.

The main reason many people buy things on credit is that they are able to have the desired or needed items sooner than if they were to wait until they had saved enough to buy such items for cash. Some people find it easier to pay for things by means of regular installment payments than to accumulate the same amount of money in a savings account. In fact, some people who have savings will use installment credit because they do not wish to reduce their savings for fear that if they do they might not build their accounts up again.

Even if you are successful in resisting the urge to "charge it" and you keep your credit purchases down to a minimum, there is still a price you pay. First, the cash price when you buy is usually higher where credit is offered. Also, the price is higher on a credit plan than if you borrowed the money from your bank or credit union and paid cash. Most charge accounts require a 1.5 percent per month interest on the unpaid part of your debt. That figures out to a rate of 18 percent per year, and that's a lot of money!

Advantages of Using Credit

There are also some advantages to a wise use of credit. Properly managed credit can stretch your dollar and help your family get far more out of life. It can help you realize more of your objectives and goals. This should be especially important to the Christian family. Here are some examples of the ways credit can increase your spending power. A farmer borrows money to buy a new tractor that will help him increase his yield. A $225 washer will eventually pay for itself if you are now paying $95 a year in quarters to use a coin-operated machine, not even counting the extra convenience. You may buy storm windows to cut heating and cooling bills, a side of beef at discount for your freezer, or a sewing machine that will enable you to make clothes for your family. Occasionally, it is possible to buy something that you really need on sale, when the sale price plus interest and carrying charges is still significantly below the original cost. Or, credit may enable you to build a needed addition to your house rather than make a costly move to a larger one.

Credit can also level out the peaks and valleys in your spending, allowing you to buy what you need during high-expense periods, such as when the children go back to school or off to college or at Christmas, while spreading payments evenly over several months.[2]

Some people expect prices to continue to rise at a rapid rate. If you have a lender whose interest doesn't go up with inflation, your loan becomes "cheaper" in a period of steep inflation.

Credit is available almost everywhere you turn—banks, finance companies, credit unions, and retail stores. Its ready availability makes it a ready liability. It is a service that dealers offer, but it costs more. Most families are completely unaware of what they pay for the use of credit. If you fail to exercise reasonable control, you pay the price, and sometimes a very heavy price, even bankruptcy. Remember, credit is like fire—*it is easy to start and very useful, but it can be extremely dangerous if you are careless with it.*[3] Therefore, it makes good sense to protect one's family, one's job, and one's future by using it for constructive purposes. Good credit is one of the most valuable assets a person has.

When you ask for credit, the lender will investigate you as a financial risk. His first concern is whether or not you will pay back what you borrow. To ease that concern they will want to know where you live, where you work, how much you make, how much you already owe, what your past record has been in paying your debts, and even your character. Once credit is established, it is a real asset—guard it!

Common Types of Credit

There are many kinds of credit. It is important to know something about the most common types. Consider these:

1. Regular charge accounts. These are offered by many department stores, specialty shops, and oil companies. They require

no down payment or prepurchase deposit. Most firms charge 1.5 percent a month interest on any unpaid balance—remember this is actually 18 percent. This can be an extremely convenient account when used as a twenty-five- to thirty-day charge without paying any interest charges. It can consolidate several bills into one; thus it will require only one check or payment. It also means that you can leave your money in the bank or in savings for this period of time. However, you must be sure to pay the bill in full when it is due.

2. *Ninety-day accounts.* These are offered mainly by specialty shops and some department and furniture stores. This account allows the bill to be paid in three monthly installments, without interest charges. This can also be a real convenience.

3. *Revolving charge accounts.* These accounts permit you to charge purchases up to a stated amount which the store has allocated to you. You are billed monthly and no interest is charged if the bill is paid in full before the due date. If you pay installments, an interest rate of 1.5 percent monthly is usually charged, based on the unpaid balance at the time of billing. Often there is a carrying charge in addition to interest charges. This costs you money and should be considered as part of your total price.

One problem here is that many people establish an account at one or two stores and become so committed to them that they are never in a position to pay cash or shop at other stores. When you are unable to shop around and compare prices you surrender one of your most effective weapons. It is especially unwise to purchase clothing and other small items on a revolving charge account. These accounts should be used with caution.

4. *Installment contracts.* These make it possible for large purchases such as a major appliance or furniture to be paid for in monthly installments. Usually, you make a down payment and sign a contract for the balance of the purchase price. Interest

rates and carrying charges on accounts of this type may range from 1.5 percent to 3.5 percent monthly to 40 percent annually. It can be a sizable amount, and it is always wise to see if it would be more economical to use a loan from your bank or credit union.

5. *Credit cards.* Approximately three hundred million credit cards are in circulation in America. Their increasing use led Senator William Proxmire of Wisconsin to comment in a speech on the Senate floor on April 15, 1970:

Look what one can do with a little plastic credit card—you can fly now, have a full vacation, and pay later; get a car fixed and finance a myriad of other personal services; stay in the finest hotels, eat at the best restaurants, enjoy top entertainment, or purchase almost any other commodity imaginable. Even things like charitable contributions can be handled by credit cards, and recently several banks announced that their credit cards can now be used to pay taxes. The plastic credit card revolution is upon us in full force. The era of the plastic card economy is fast approaching.[4]

Bank credit cards and oil company credit cards have no initial cost and require no annual fee. These can be very useful when bills are paid promptly and no interest is paid. However, credit through credit cards is becoming so "easy" that financial ruin is simply a matter of presenting that shiny plastic card once too often for many people. Some families fall into the trap of using credit cards for impulse buying. Many merchants estimate that as much as 70 percent of their goods are bought on impulse. How many of these purchases end up on a closet shelf after a single use or two? Advance planning will help you avoid buying what you don't really need. Using a credit card can become an insidious disease. Avoid competitive living. Think before you buy!

Prices may be higher at stores that use credit cards. These stores pay the credit card company from 3 percent to 5 percent of everything their card-carrying customers charge. They tend to raise their prices about this amount too.

If a credit card is lost or stolen, you can be held liable for the first $50 of charges on it if it is used before you report the loss. If something happens to a credit card, notify the company by telephone and follow up with a letter or telegram, making reference to your previous call.

Three good rules to follow to protect yourself in the use of credit cards are:

1. Go over every card you now own and destroy any that you do not use. Cut them in pieces or burn them.

2. Make a list of all credit cards you keep, with the name and address of each issuer and the account number. Keep this information in some safe place other than your wallet or purse.

3. Be sure you sign all your cards properly, to avoid an invitation to forgery of your signature if the card is lost.

Shop for Your Credit Source

In addition to the five sources of credit listed, it is also possible to obtain cash loans from credit unions, banks, savings and loan associations, and small loan companies. Credit costs vary greatly on personal loans depending on the way interest is figured and the place where you obtain the loan. Usually, credit unions and banks charge the lowest interest rates and small loan companies the largest. This is often based on your credit references, which emphasizes the importance of maintaining a good credit record.

You can also borrow on your life insurance, up to 95 percent of the cash value in most cases, at the low rate spelled out in the policy. This is usually from 5 percent to 6 percent simple interest. One problem is that you are not under a set repayment plan, and you may find it difficult to discipline yourself to repay the loan. In the meantime, the dollar cost mounts up, and your family's benefits are reduced by this amount should anything happen before the loan is repaid.

The important thing to remember is to always shop around for the least expensive credit source! The amount you save on credit may be more than you save on the price of a "bargain" purchase. Look at the difference in cost on the purchase of a major home appliance using various finance plans.

If you are going to shop intelligently for credit, you need to know what that credit is actually costing you. One simple

FIVE WAYS TO FINANCE THE PURCHASE OF A MAJOR HOME APPLIANCE—AT FIVE DIFFERENT COSTS

Cost of Refrigerator/Freezer: $362.71	Loan Against Life Insurance Policy Cash Value @ 5%	Collateral Bank Loan @ 8%	Bank Installment Loan	Department Store Charge Card	Finance Co. Installment Loan
Amount Borrowed	$362.71	$362.71	$362.71	$362.71	$362.71
Term of Loan	Not applicable	Not applicable	24 months	Not applicable	24 months
Monthly Payments	None	None	$ 17.83	5% or $10.00*	$ 20.00
Annual Percentage Rate	5.3%	8.0%	17.3%	18.0%	31.0%
Type of Interest or Periodic Rate	Discount Rate	Simple Interest	Discount Rate	1½% monthly on 1st $1,000	2½% monthly on 1st $200. 2% over $200
Total Interest Paid Over 2-Year Period	$ 39.13	$ 58.04 (collected quarterly)	$ 65.21	*	$117.29
Total Sum to Be Repaid Over 2-Year Period	$401.84	$420.75	$427.92	*	$480.00

*It is customary for banks and department stores to assess an annual percentage rate of 18% on unpaid balances up to and including $1,000. Minimum monthly payment schedules usually call for payments of $10 monthly on balance owed of $10 to $200 and 5% of new balances over $200. Late charges total from $1.00 minimum to $5.00 maximum. Because of the flexible nature of these plans it is not practical to simulate an account showing total sum repaid or total interest charged over a 2-year period.

(This chart is taken from booklet "How Much Do I Owe? How Much Can I Borrow? A Personal Analysis and Guide." The Dreyfus Family Money Management Service, pp. 10-11.)

method is to add up all the costs, then subtract the cash price of what you are buying. In the illustration of the refrigerator/freezer, the difference was from a low of $39.13 to a high of $117.29. That's a difference of $78.16 and that is well worth shopping for!

The Federal Truth in Lending Act of 1968 requires anyone who lends money or provides credit to explain, as a simple percentage, the price you'll pay for the credit costs and the services or finance charge. This information is important to you as you shop for credit. However, you should remember that the simple percentage is not the true annual rate. You can use the following rule-of-thumb as a general guide: When charges are based on the original amount owed and included in twelve monthly installments, the true yearly rate is approximately double. With the following chart you can quickly determine the true annual rate of interest:

What Interest Rates Really Mean

When Charged	True Annual Rate
5% a year or $ 4 per $100	9.2
6% a year or $ 6 per $100	10.9
8% a year or $ 8 per $100	14.5
10% a year or $10 per $100	18.0

If an interest rate is quoted only on an unpaid amount owed, a general guide is to multiply the monthly percentage by 12 to get the true annual rate:

1% per month on unpaid balance	12
1.25% per month on unpaid balance	15
1.5% per month on unpaid balance	18
2% per month on unpaid balance	24

Money management experts say there are five secrets to using credit at the lowest cost. They are:

1. Borrow from the source where you can get the lowest true

annual rate, not from the source that is the handiest or quickest.

2. Borrow the least you need, not the most you can get.

3. Make your monthly payments as large as you can, not as small as the lender will permit.

4. Repay the loan in as short a period as possible, not as long as you can arrange it.

5. Do not borrow unnecessarily, and do not borrow far in advance of the actual need.[5]

Know When and How to Use Credit

When it becomes necessary for you to use credit, you will have to answer the question, How much? You should remember that you are vulnerable when your liquid assets are not enough to meet emergencies and you are over-committed on credit payments. Since families have different values and needs, there is no easy formula. Before you decide on a major credit purchase or loan, look at your total family financial picture. Preview your spending for the coming year. Use the records in the notebook you have been keeping as a guide. What's your monthly income? What are your regular expenses? What's left for savings or careful spending? Check your credit commitments, month by month, and see if there is room now for another debt. Will there be in a few months? If so, be selective when you do borrow or buy on credit.

If you've never been able to save, you should have some very good idea of where you're going to find the money to make payments before you undertake a loan. And, of course, if you're now struggling to pay off what you owe, you should avoid the temptation to take on new debts as you would a disease.

The average middle-class American family should probably take on no more than 20 percent of its net income, excluding a home mortgage, for installment payments. This is only an estimate. Your family finance records may indicate that it is possible for you to go beyond the 20 percent, or they may indicate that you should stay well below that percentage.

Whenever you borrow money or make a credit purchase, you are usually required to sign a contract. Never sign such a contract without first reading and understanding its terms. To do so without reading it is as dangerous and foolish as signing a blank check. If you do not understand it, have some qualified person explain it to you. A contract states the mutual obligation of the buyer and the seller. The wording will always protect the seller, so you must be sure that it also protects you. Some stores write into their contracts a pledge of all your resalable household goods, not just a pledge of what you are buying now. That means that if you fail to make the payments on the new purchase, they can repossess it along with your other household furnishings.

Be sure that the interest rates, insurance fees, or any other parts of the total cost are itemized separately. Pay special attention to the finance charges—know what you are paying for. Also be sure that all blank spaces are filled in and all amounts are listed correctly. Be sure that you are dealing with a reputable dealer and that he will stand behind all products. Often dealers sell their contracts to a loan company who is only interested in collecting the debt—not whether the new purchase works. See if the contract allows you to refuse merchandise which is defective or is not as promised.

Some contracts contain a "balloon payment." This means that a series of small payments are made, followed by a large sum that ends the indebtedness. Make sure you know what that amount is. Can you get a refund of interest or carrying charges if you complete payments ahead of time? This is good to know as it can save you some money. Also see if the contract calls for a penalty for late payments. This can amount to 5 percent or more of the payment. As long as you make your payments, this clause will not affect you. But if you fail to make your payments on time, it can add an extra financial burden.

People borrow money to buy things or do things. Other people lend money to *make* money. They make this money off of the borrower. If you use your credit wisely, you can often stretch your dollar and help your family get more out of life. Good credit is one of your most valuable assets. Use it wisely!

For Your Consideration

1. *Name some of the advantages you have when you buy with cash.*
2. *What are some of the advantages in using credit?*
3. *List at least five different common types of credit along with their advantages or disadvantages.*
4. *What are three good rules to follow to protect yourself in the use of credit cards?*
5. *Why is it important to shop around for credit?*
6. *What is probably* your *best source of credit or cash loan?*
7. *List some of the things you should remember to find out before you sign a contract.*

Notes

1. Reprinted from the book *How to Stretch Your Income*, Copyright 1971 U.S. News & World Report, Inc., Washington, D.C. 20037.

2. *Ibid.*, p. 33.

3. *Ibid.*, p. 31.

4. A speech by Senator William Proxmire made on the Senate floor April 15, 1970.

5. *Ibid.*, pp. 39-41

7.
RESPONSIBLE CHRISTIAN GIVING

(Achieving Greatness in Giving)

Have you ever parked at a parking meter that had time left on it? Someone put a coin in the meter and left before the time ran out. You came along and got to park on the other person's nickel. Every church has people who "park on the other person's nickel." They do not give to finance the ministries of the church, but they receive the benefits. Parking on the other person's nickel at the parking meter is not a serious matter; parking on the other person's gift to the church is.

Old Testament Teachings

Any examination of what constitutes responsible Christian giving must begin with a consideration of what the Bible says. Throughout the Old Testament the concept of the *tithe* was predominant. The word *tithe* means "the tenth." As a religious practice, tithing may be defined as the giving of a tenth of the annual produce or other income, less the cost of producing that income, for the support of a particular religious ministry.

The first recorded instance of payment of a tithe is the offering of Abraham to Melchizedek (Gen. 14:1-20). Abraham had defeated an alliance of kings who had looted Sodom and had taken captive Abraham's nephew Lot and his family. As they returned from the victorious battle with all the loot and the people, Abraham was met by the king of Sodom and Melchizedek, king of Salem, a priest of God. Abraham gave Melchizedek a tenth of everything—not because of Melchizedek's ownership, but because he served as the priest of God, the true owner of man's possessions.

The second time the tithe is mentioned is in the promise Jacob made to God in the light of his realization of God's presence at Bethel. Jacob promised that if God remained in his life, he would give God a tenth of all his increase (Gen. 28:10-22).

There were at least three distinct tithes in the Old Testament. The first was known as the Lord's or the Levite's, the whole tithe. It consisted of one tenth annually, whether of the seed of the land, the fruit of the tree, the herd or the flock. This tithe supported the Levitical priesthood (Lev. 27:30-32).

The second tithe was given to support three great feasts—Passover, Tabernacles, and Weeks. Travel and other expenses during the pilgrims' stay in Jerusalem were taken from this tithe.

Every three years a third tithe was given (Deut. 12:5-19; 14:22-27). It was kept in local communities for distribution to the needy (Deut. 14:28-29). The two annual tithes and the third-year tithe amounted to about one fourth of one's income.

Many Israelities disobeyed God in their failure to bring the tithe as commanded. Of particular interest is Malachi's solemn accusation that the people of his day were guilty of robbing God by their refusal to pay tithes and give offerings.

New Testament Teachings

Jesus' teachings in the New Testament present quite a different story. Although approximately one sixth of Jesus' teaching deals with the attitude of a person toward his possessions, he never mentioned the tithe in his teachings. The two times Jesus did mention tithing were negative pronouncements related to Jewish legalistic piety (Luke 18:12; Matt. 23:23).

Jesus did not ask for a tithe or a proportion. He asked only that we give "freely" (Matt. 10:8). If Jesus had established definite rules requiring a tenth or any other proportion of our incomes, the force of his teachings about possessing and giving would have been *weakened*.

Jesus never condemned the careful stewardship reflected in tithing. He did condemn a sense of values that had lost correct perspective where God's law of possessions was concerned. Jesus understood that the tithe was meant to teach God's total ownership. Just as the land and all that it produced belonged to God, so man in his totality belonged to God. All of man was to be used for God. Likewise, all of man's possessions should be used for God's glory. Nowhere in the New Testament does it suggest that we give less than a tenth. Jesus didn't die on the cross so that man could do less instead of more.

The only other references to tithing in the New Testament are in Hebrew 7. These are really a part of the larger argument for the preeminence of Christ. They have no bearing on the question of stewardship in the early church. When the Holy Spirit took charge of the church on the day of Pentecost, the members began to consider their responsibility with reference to properties. Luke wrote: "All that believed were together, and had all things common; and sold their possessions and goods, and parted them to all men, as every man had need" (Acts 2:44-45).

John and James in their letters urged giving to meet human needs (1 John 3:17; Jas. 2:15-16). Paul was also interested in the matter of giving. He was part of a movement to raise funds for the poor of the church in Jerusalem. With reference to this particular movement and somewhat as general instructions, he said, "Upon the first day of the week let every one of you lay by him in store, as God has prospered him" (1 Cor. 16:2). Four things stand out in this: (1) Everyone was to give. (2) The gifts were to be stored before the needs of the poor had been met.

(3) The giving was according to prosperity. (4) The giving was to be done every Lord's Day.

We might conclude from what the Bible says that the Christian is not subject to the Mosaic law—neither is he to be lawless in his behavior—he is subject to Christ! This does not prevent the Christian from tithing, but we should understand that the New Testament does not command a tithe. If a Christian decides in his heart that he will give a tenth of his income to the Lord, he is free to do so and will find the practice highly rewarding.

In his book *A Christian and His Money,* John R. Crawford says of the tithe: "Nor can we say, as some would like to say in genuine sincerity, that a person who begins tithing is guaranteed to prosper materially. God guarantees us his love, his concern, his presence, and the possibility of reconciliation to him with a new life to follow. He does not promise us that if we tithe we shall have a handsome bank account or a life freed from fiscal problems. Tithers have gone bankrupt; nontithers have been known to prosper by completely legal means." [1]

The Christian should not tithe from a sense of legal obligation, with the expectation of great financial gain in return, or with the idea that the tithe is the full measure of his response to the call of Christian stewardship. Neither should he feel that the other nine-tenths are his to use as he pleases. Tithing should be only a small part of the larger doctrine of stewardship. The principle behind the tithe, the recognition of God's ownership of all of life, is still applicable to every Christian. It is basically an act of worship that declares the greatness of God and the worth of man when he is obedient to God.

The Christian Standard of Giving

The Christian standard of giving is based on the supreme self-giving of God through Jesus Christ. Christian stewardship must flow from an understanding of what God has done for us. We give out of hearts full of thanksgiving and love. Had God set a definite amount, most of us would do no more. Love compels us to soar to new heights in giving, going beyond the requirements of law. Love will not allow the Christian to be content to "park on the other man's nickel."

Christian giving, then, finds its motives, objectives, and dimensions in one's personal relationship to Christ. Our purpose in giving is important. In commending the Corinthians for their liberality in the Jerusalem offering, Paul gave a brief, inclusive statement: "Under the test of this service, you will glorify God by your obedience in acknowledging the gospel of Christ, and by the generosity of your contribution for them and for all others" (2 Cor. 9:13, RSV). Here three important purposes of giving are spelled out: (1) to glorify God, (2) to serve man, and (3) to discipline the self.

The first purpose of giving is to glorify God. This acknowledges the sovereignty of God in the universe and as the source of all blessings of life.

The second purpose of giving is to serve the needs of man. The Hebrews gave of their tithes and various gifts of charity to serve the needs of people. In the New Testament a major purpose of giving is to lessen human problems. Jesus said that when we give to men in need, we give to the Lord himself (Matt. 25:31-46).

The third purpose of giving is to discipline the self. The foundation of stewardship is the affirmation that "The earth is the Lord's and the fulness thereof, the world and those who dwell therein" (Ps. 24:1, RSV). As we give, we are reminded that God is the owner of all our resources, and we are stewards who must give an account to him. We are to be liberal in our sharing with others that we may lay up treasures in heaven.

Motives for Giving

A study of the Scriptures further reveals that the motives for giving are varied. Some motives are intensely self-centered and appeal to selfish ambitions. Others are Christ-centered and produce acts of devotion and love.

Motives are important because they determine the spiritual value of giving. Consider these motives for giving:

1. *To prosper.* This is one of the dominant motivations to giving in the Old Testament. This approach is dominated by the idea that riches are a sign of God's blessings and are a reward for faithfulness. (See Deut. 8:18; Prov. 3:9-10; Mal. 3:10.)

2. *To gain God's favor.* This is a second motive evident in Old Testament giving. (See Gen. 28:20-21; Isa. 1:11.)

3. *To remove spiritual barriers.* In the New Testament Jesus challenged the rich young man to give in order to remove the things that prevented him from coming to Jesus. (See Matt. 19:16-22.)

4. *To right wrongs.* Zacchaeus gave half of all he had to the poor and used another part to correct the wrong he had done to others (Luke 19:1-10). The account shows Jesus' attitude toward wealth wrongly gained and reflects his dual concern for a man's ministry to others.

5. *To share in furthering the gospel.* Paul was grateful for those who had supported him through their material gifts and, thus, had a part in his ministry and furthering the gospel. (See Phil. 1:3-5.)

6. *To express love and gratitude.* This is the highest motive for giving. In reality, this is the one truly Christian motive. Paul said that the Jerusalem gift was proof before the churches of genuine love. (See 2 Cor. 8:8,24.)

Few people would argue that part of what the Christian earns should be given to the church. But such questions usually arise as: How much? How shall I decide? How should my life-style affect my giving? These questions are not easily answered. They involve very personal matters. In most definitions of stewardship, we find the words *systematic* and *proportionate* used. A clue to the answer to these questions is found in these words. What we give should certainly be a part of a regular "system," not simply an occasional outburst caused by either generosity or guilt. As a normal part of life, we eat to sustain our bodies and observe certain periods of time for sleep to restore them. We ask God to "give us this day our daily bread" (Matt. 6:11) and depend upon him to do it. Therefore, it seems only fair that our "systematic giving" should be our response to God's systematic provision for all of our needs. The word *proportionate* means something that is related to our income and our other needs. Therefore, our giving to our church should be related to the rest of our life.

Principles of Giving

It is probably unwise to try to set up elaborate rules for our giving based on proof texts. However, there are certain principles that run throughout the Bible, despite differences in detailed application. The following principles are among those that should guide us.

1. *Seek the kingdom of God first* (Matt. 6:33). This is life's first priority. When the Christian obeys this, everything else falls into its proper place, including responsible giving.

2. *Give yourself first.* In biblical thought, the giver is identified with his gift. Paul said that before the Macedonian Christians contributed to the Jerusalem offering they "first . . . gave themselves to the Lord and to us" (2 Cor. 8:5, RSV).

3. *Give as God prospers.* The basis of Old Testament tithing was proportionate giving. The New Testament removes giving from a legal basis but retains the idea of the individual giving as God has prospered him. See what Paul said about this in 2 Corinthians 8:12.

4. *Give the first and best to God.* The Old Testament system required the firstfruits and the best animals of harvest for God

(Ex. 22:29-30; Deut. 17:1; Mal. 1:6-8). As one gives God first priority, he also dedicates the remainder of his resources to God's service. Remember your listing of fixed expenses? Church contributions were listed first. They are that important!

5. *Give systematically.* The Old Testament tithing system assured regular patterns of giving. Paul instructed the Corinthians to put something aside and store it up on the first day of the week (1 Cor. 16:2). Giving should not be a hit and miss proposition.

6. *Give generously.* New Testament liberality of love superceded Old Testament legalism. Generosity, not percentage rules, becomes the guiding principle. Paul said the generous gifts overflowed in a wealth of liberality (2 Cor. 8:2; 9:11).

7. *Give voluntarily.* Old Testament legal obligation is unworthy for the Christian. The only gift that honors God comes from a willing, loving heart. Read what Paul said about this in 2 Corinthians 9:7.

8. *Give spontaneously.* Immediate needs often require spontaneous response. Giving to the poor was hallowed by Jewish tradition and emphasized by Jesus. No amount of systematic, proportionate giving can offset failure to give personal help as worthy needs arise.[2]

Charitable Contributions

The question often arises, "What about giving to charitable organizations outside my church?" This is not an easy question to answer. The following guidelines will help you make your own decision.

The ministries of your church should come first. If we fail to support our churches, they will die. Through our churches we have a part in ministering to the needs of people around the world. Many independent organizations require high overhead expenses and well-paid staffs that earn far more than our pastors and church staff members.

Many Christians first determine the portion of their money, such as the tithe, which they will give to their church. Then, their other contributions are figured over and above this amount. These contributions are then divided among the various civic and charitable appeals, and even among special offerings taken in the church.

Pick out those organizations and charities which you feel are particularly crucial, or those which you especially want to support. These are probably complementary to the ministries supported through your church. Evaluate them carefully to find which have a positive and lasting value, and those which are doing a unique job. Any questionable organizations or charities, or any which works contrary to the beliefs of your church, should not be supported by Christians.

Here are some guidelines from the Council of Better Business Bureaus to help you spend your charitable dollars wisely:

1. If you don't know anything about the charity, check with your local Better Business Bureau, Chamber of Commerce, or state or local consumer protection agency to see if any complaints have been registered against it.

2. Be certain the charity complies with any state or local laws.

3. Always write a check to the organization, never to the individual soliciting for the charity; never contribute in cash.

4. Check to see what the organization is doing in your own community. (Some national charities insist that local chapters send up to 75 percent of their collections to national headquarters, leaving little for community use.)

5. Demand a full accounting of the funds used. While some charities have a good record on program spending, others spend as little as 15 percent of program services. The rest ends up in the pockets of professional fund-raisers or collecting agencies rather than helping the sick, needy, or poor.

6. Get full information on who is able to participate in the benefits the charity says it is offering to people.

7. Make sure the charity is tax-exempt, nonprofit. If it isn't, your contribution won't be tax-deductible. (Some profit-making organizations hire handicapped people to collect from innocent contributors.)

8. Remember that unordered, unwanted merchandise does not have to be paid for or returned. You can use it, give it away, or throw it away—but you don't have to pay for it.

The Council of Better Business Bureaus will provide information on individual charities; you are asked to limit your queries to three to five per letter. They'll give you a rundown on the charities you specify. Write to Philanthropic Advisory Department, CBBB, 1150 17th Street, N. W., Washington, D. C. 20036.[3]

Seek God's guidance. Make your plans for all giving according to the guidelines you find in the Scriptures. Then give as you feel God would have you give.

Greatness in Giving

Christian giving finds its motives, its objectives, and its dimensions in one's personal relationship to Jesus Christ—in response to his *calling* to discipleship. Here again, the phrase *life-style* is of primary importance. We talked about this in the first chapter. Now let's take a look at some specifics related to just how a Christian might reflect his commitment to the lordship of Christ through his life-style.

We have already concluded that for the Christian, life has distinctive purposes, meanings, and ideals. Therefore, his life-style must assure his ability to demonstrate his faith and to claim unique Christian opportunities through his giving. Are you willing to undertake a self-examination of your own life-style? It may not be easy. You may be very pleased with what you discover, or you may not like it at all. However, the study should help you decide just how well you are claiming the opportunities God has given you.

Let's examine three areas: (1) your standard-of-living level, (2) your advantage level, and (3) your opportunity-giving level. For this study we need to understand that "advantage means opportunity." *Advantage money* is the income a family receives beyond the normal requirements of a reasonable standard of living. *Opportunities* refer to the new capacities to serve that come to the Christian as the result of financial advantages.

First of all, examine your standard-of-living level.

My Standard-of-Living Level

(Check the statement that best describes your standard of living.)

_____ Strongly Christian

_____ Shows some Christian influences

_____ Shows mostly the influence of my neighbors and friends

Life for the Christian has distinctive purposes, meanings, and ideals. Each believer should ask, "Is this distinctive kind of life reflected in my standard of living?"

I. *How Christian are my basic life patterns?*

	Yes	In some ways	No
1. My money rivals God's place in my life	——	——	——
2. My purposes for life are God's purposes for me	——	——	——
3. My way of earning money is under God's control	——	——	——
4. My spending habits reflect a love for Christ and his work	——	——	——
5. My income increases have helped me to be more committed to Christ's work	——	——	——
6. My financial plans for the future (insurance, wills, etc.) indicates a Christian commitment	——	——	——

II. *How Christian have been my major purchases?*

	A move into a higher standard of living	Not a luxury—but a necessary item for service
1. My last house	_____	_____
2. My last automobile	_____	_____
3. My last 3 other major purchases		
(1) _____	_____	_____
(2) _____	_____	_____
(3) _____	_____	_____

III. *How Christian is my involvement in recreation and pleasure?*

    1. List the last 4 adult "toys" purchased (hobbies, vacation, boats, lake house, golf clubs, club membership, season tickets, etc.)

        (1) _____ $_____

        (2) _____ $_____

        (3) _____ $_____

        (4) _____ $_____

    2. How does my cost for pleasure and recreation compare with my giving to Christian causes?

    The total for pleasure and recreation is equal to

    _____ 1/10, _____ ½, _____ same, _____ 2 times, _____ 3 times or more than my total for giving.

IV. *How Christian is my installment buying pattern?*

My payments compared to my giving are:

	½	Equal	2 times	3 times	More
1. My house payments	___	___	___	___	___
2. My car payments	___	___	___	___	___
3. My other installment payments	___	___	___	___	___
4. My interest payments on debts	___	___	___	___	___

V. *How Christian is my use of my advantage money?*

Advantage money refers primarily to the increases in income that allow the family to make choices about new opportunities in life.

I use my advantage money to:

_____ upgrade my standard living

_____ increase my service to my family (present and future)

_____ increase my support of church ministries

_____ to serve people in need

VI. *How Christian is my commitment level?*

	Yes	Somewhat	No
1. I am happy with: my present income	——	————	——
my present house	——	————	——
my way of life	——	————	——
2. I would be happier with: more income	——	————	——
a larger house	——	————	——
more luxuries	——	————	——

3. How much money is enough for me (annual income) $_____

4. To what extent am I willing to allow the claims of the lordship of Christ to affect my standard of living?

_____ completely _____ some _____ none

My Advantage Level

Advantage money is the income that one receives in excess of the basic needs of sustaining life—food, clothes, shelter, medicine, transportation, and a reasonable standard of living. Figure to see how much advantage money you really have and how this compares percentage wise to your other expenses.

My total income for the year is $_____.

My life necessities amount to $_____ or _____ % of total.

Include enough for food, clothes, housing, medicine, transportation, and other needs to sustain life. Add up your present cost for these, then reduce the total to the amount the family could survive on. This is your necessity level. What percentage is it of your total income?

My reasonable standard of living is $＿＿＿＿＿＿ or ＿＿＿ % of total.

Include necessities plus reasonable allowances for comfort, education, and culture. It may be necessary to figure as if you were planning for less expensive housing, car, recreation, etc. Compare your estimate with the cost-of-living estimate for your community. What percentage is this to your total income?

My advantage money is $＿＿＿＿＿＿ or ＿＿＿% of total.

Include all income beyond the reasonable standard-of-living costs. Advantage money allows for special opportunities in life.

What do I do with advantage money?

1. What has been my purpose for advantage money?

   (1)＿＿＿＿＿＿＿＿＿＿   (4) ＿＿＿＿＿＿＿＿＿＿＿
   (2)＿＿＿＿＿＿＿＿＿＿   (5) ＿＿＿＿＿＿＿＿＿＿＿
   (3)＿＿＿＿＿＿＿＿＿＿   (6) ＿＿＿＿＿＿＿＿＿＿＿

2. Do the ways I have been using advantage money reflect my Christian commitment?   Yes ＿＿＿＿   No ＿＿＿＿

3. What special kinds of opportunities in life should my advantage money make possible?

   (1)＿＿＿＿＿＿＿＿＿＿   (3) ＿＿＿＿＿＿＿＿＿＿＿
   (2)＿＿＿＿＿＿＿＿＿＿   (4) ＿＿＿＿＿＿＿＿＿＿＿

4. What opportunities will I set as my goal for the future?

   (1)＿＿＿＿＿＿＿＿＿＿   (3) ＿＿＿＿＿＿＿＿＿＿＿
   (2)＿＿＿＿＿＿＿＿＿＿   (4) ＿＿＿＿＿＿＿＿＿＿＿

My Opportunity Giving Level

Advantage money brings added opportunities that have special meaning for the Christian. One opportunity of great importance is growth in responsible Christian giving.

I. What is my present opportunity-giving level?

I now give ＿＿＿% of my reasonable standard $＿＿＿＿＿
of living   (amount given)

I now give ＿＿＿% of my advantage money $＿＿＿＿＿
                                                         (amount given)

II. *My goal for the future in opportunity-giving*

Taking into consideration your commitment to Christ and your desire to develop a life-style that reflects that commitment, use the following work-space to develop your own systematic plan for growth in Christian giving.

I will give ____% of my reasonable standard of living $_____

I will give ____% of 1st $1,000 of advantage money   _____

I will give ____% of 2nd $1,000 of advantage money   _____

I will give ____% of 3rd $1,000 of advantage money   _____

I will give ____% of 4th $1,000 of advantage money   _____

I will give ____% of 5th $1,000 of advantage money etc.   _____

Total $_____

Examples

1. One family with an annual income of $14,000 adopted $8,500 as their reasonable standard of living level and decided to give 10% of this part and then to increase by 1% for each extra $1,000 of advantage money.

10% of $8,500	=	$ 850
11% of next $1,000	=	110
12% of next $1,000	=	120
13% of next $1,000	=	130
14% of next $1,000	=	140
15% of next $1,000	=	150
16% of next $ 500	=	80
Total		$1,580

2. A second family with an income of $16,000 felt that a $10,000 level was a more reasonable standard of living, and they started their giving growth where they were, at 8%. They then decided to increase their gifts by 2% for each $1,000 of advantage money.

8% of $10,000	=	$ 800
10% of next $1,000	=	100
12% of next $1,000	=	120
14% of next $1,000	=	140
16% of next $1,000	=	160
18% of next $1,000	=	180
20% of next $1,000	=	200
Total		$1,700

Well, what do you think? You may already be doing far greater than anything suggested by this study. On the other hand, the study may have shown you that there is some room for improvement in your own giving.

Remember, the Christian standard of giving is based on the supreme self-giving in light of biblical standards. Examine your own personal response. No amount is too much in light of all that God has provided. Dare to strive for greatness in your giving.

For Your Consideration

1. *What is the teaching concerning the tithe in the Old and New Testaments?*
2. *What four things stand out in Paul's teaching concerning giving?*
3. *Upon what is the Christian standard of giving based?*
4. *Paul mentioned three purposes for giving, what are they?*
5. *Which of the principles which should guide Christian giving are the most meaningful to you?*
7. *In the study of your own life-style, what decisions did you reach in regard to your own growth in Christian giving?*

Notes

1. This section is taken from my own writing as published in *Source,* October-December, 1973, pages 51-60. Basic resource for this was *Resource Unlimited.*

2. "Everybody's Money," Autumn '74, Credit Union National Association, Box 431, Madison, Wisconsin 53701.

3. The section on "Greatness in Giving," is taken from an unpublished work paper provided by Cecil Ray, director of Church Stewardship Department, Baptist General Convention of Texas, and is used here by his permission.

8.
CHILDREN AND THEIR MONEY
(Using It and Abusing It!)

In these days of high cost and big spending, it wouldn't surprise many parents if the first word the baby spoke was *money*. Long before a child can begin to earn money, he is spending it—either directly through his own form of management or indirectly through the management of his parents. Maria, two years old, can just toddle behind her mother in the supermarket, but she is already aware of the gum-ball economy in which she lives. If she puts a penny in the gum-ball machine, out comes a brightly colored ball of gum. On every shopping trip with her mother she demands her penny for the machine. Eight-year-old Melinda is in the third grade. She gets a weekly allowance to pay for school lunches, extra milk, school supplies, and fifty cents of her very own to spend as she wishes. Both girls are spending, although their understanding of the use of money is quite different.

Examine Your Own Attitudes

Children are not born with the ability to manage money wisely. They learn from experience and example, and the process is a long one. Many parents are unaware that the spending and saving attitudes developed by children are essentially those that they will carry with them into adolescence and adulthood. That is why certain basics about the wise use of money must be taught to children. On shopping trips, children observe their parents handing the clerk at the counter pieces of green paper and shiny objects shaped like pennies. In exchange, the parents take sacks of food, clothing, or perhaps some new appliance. Through observation, children become aware of the important role that money plays in the lives of their parents. They hear the value of money discussed around them. They come to understand that the reason Daddy goes to work is to earn money. They learn something of the value we place on its possession by the way we talk about it and how we use it. First impressions come from parents, other adults, and older brothers and sisters. Other impressions force themselves in from every side. Highly developed sales techniques in most radio and television commercials keep children under constant pressure to buy such items as breakfast cereals, toys, and the latest style clothing.

Since the spending and saving attitudes developed by children are basically those that they will carry with them all of their lives, it, therefore, becomes doubly important that throughout their developmental years we instill into them the proper attitudes about money and how it should be used. Giving children a sense of values about money matters is one of the primary responsibilities of every parent.

Children learn from adult attitudes and examples. Before you can help your child develop the proper attitudes toward money, you need to examine the values which you place on it. Your answers to the following questions are important as you attempt to influence the attitudes of your children: What value do I place on money? Do I tend to measure the worth of everything, including people, in terms of money? In my own childhood, how were my attitudes toward money influenced by my parents? How does my background with respect to money matters compare with that of my wife (or husband)? Do I discuss money matters openly and realistically with the entire family? What do I see as the primary purpose of my money?

It is also important to realize that it doesn't necessarily follow that children will adopt their parents' attitudes. In fact, a child may have an opposite reaction. A very stingy father may have an unusually generous fourteen-year-old son. In another family, the parents may not only be free with their money, they may be extremely careless with it. Yet, their eleven-year-old daughter hates to spend a cent and can make her dollar-a-week allowance last a month. Her excess is a reaction to her parents' excesses in the opposite direction.[1]

Whether a child's attitude toward money is the same as the parents or opposite from theirs, the important fact is that the attitudes of the parents do have a powerful influence. This is particularly true when children are small. In his book *The Christian Man's World*, Robert Hastings has said: "The weight of a single leaf on moist cement, freshly poured, will make a lasting impression.

"Once the concrete has hardened, sledge hammer blows are required to do what a single leaf could have done earlier. Likewise, a great deal of time spent with children when they are older will not make up for the lost opportunities when they were young." [2]

Because money matters are closely involved with family relationships, we must be extremely careful that they do not create added problems in family life. Parents usually find that good financial relationships with their children help develop better emotional relationships within the family also. This points up the value of including children in family financial discussions. The parents who seem to be doing the best job of developing sound attitudes toward money with their children have made them a part of the family financial planning.

The finest education in the use of money comes from sharing sessions when the family sits down together and talks freely about using their income in the best possible way for the good of all. This gives everyone a sense of security, confidence, and fairness. When children are brought into the family discussions as soon as they are mature enough to contribute ideas, both parents and children learn to appreciate each other's needs in relation to the needs of the entire family. Many parents control all of the spending of family money far too long, because they are timid about letting their children in on it. This is a natural reaction when family income is limited and all spending must be carefully guarded. However, it is a poor way to train children for the day when they will be managing their own income.

Begin with an Allowance

Children can and should learn to manage money. Money is a tool; and as is true of all tools, learning to use it requires practice in handling it. About the time a child starts to school, he is ready to learn something about handling money of his own. By letting him begin early with small amounts, you can avoid costly mistakes that neither you as a parent or the child can afford. One of the best tools to learn to handle money wisely is through an allowance. A reasonable, weekly allowance provides an opportunity for teaching evaluation, good judgment, budgeting, and self-reliance. Over the years a child can learn how to live within his income, how to purchase selectively, how to care for future wants or needs, how to give, and even how to do without. The amount a child receives should depend upon family circumstances and the child's needs—not on the amount of the allowances of his friends.

Some parents are reluctant to begin giving their children a regular allowance. Often, parents do not realize how much they are giving out in nickels, dimes, and quarters to satisfy special requests.

Paul, a twelve-year-old grade school student, recently bought a fifteen-dollar transistor radio. He had wanted it for several months. Paul received a regular weekly allowance and had saved patiently for the radio. A friend of his, David, did not receive an allowance. He wanted a radio like Paul's. His parents would not give him the money to buy it. Actually, in the course of a few months, David received more money from his parents for various expenses than Paul did; but it was irregular, and David never had an opportunity to learn how to budget or save.

An allowance should be understood to be the child's to do with as he likes. The amount should be given regularly with no extras. Some agreement may be reached on certain "must" items (such as money for church and school lunches), but with the rest he can spend it, save it, give it away, waste it, or lose it. It is important to let the child make mistakes with his own money. That is how he learns. Parents need the courage to see a child's allowance and the way he uses it as a definite contribution to character development, not simply in terms of the things it buys or fails to buy.

In planning an allowance, the child's age should be considered as well as what items the allowance is supposed to cover. To the eight-year-old in the third grade, $3.50 a week to cover lunches, school supplies, and an additional amount for his own desires, may be sufficient. But as children grow, their interests broaden and their outside social activities demand more money. Most fares and admissions increase after the age twelve. The allowance, plus what might be earned on a part-time job, should be reconsidered from time to time and adjusted to fit the individual need. When boys and girls enter their early teens, they need the experience of making more serious decisions for themselves. Here again, there should be some understanding about what the allowance should cover such as clothes, dates, school expenses, grooming aids, and recreation. They are rapidly approaching greater responsibility and greater independence as they near adulthood.

Learning to give is also an important aspect of a child's development. Even at an early age a child can tell the difference between a gift given with real meaning, and possibly sacrifice, and a gift given carelessly. When a child has a weekly allowance of fifty cents, and gives ten cents of his own money to Sunday School or your church's offering every week, he will quickly learn that he is really giving up something that he could buy for himself in order to do this. On the other hand, if you provide your child with his weekly offering, whether it be ten cents or a dollar, his gift will be given without much meaning because it is not really his to give. It is really your gift and he merely passes it on as he has been instructed to do. Any gift which comes from his own limited income will make much more of an impression on him and will help him develop the capacity to share with others in their need.

Learning To Use Money Wisely

As children mature, it is important to help them see the need for developing a budget and keeping a record of how they have used their money. The chapter on "Why and How to Build a Budget" can provide good guidance. Some parents insist that their children keep accurate records of everything they spend. Children find this to be a boring and tedious task. It is probably better to wait until they are old enough to realize the importance of keeping a record before this is required. When they begin to realize themselves how easily the allowance or money they have earned slips away, they will become interested in keeping track of expenditures for their own information.

Children may sometime want or need to buy something which costs more than their weekly allowance can take care of, a pair of skates for example. Sometimes the solution is simply to save each week until the needed amount is in hand. However, the question of borrowing from parents or each other will often arise. Occasional borrowing against future allowances gives you a ready-made opening to teach the fundamentals of credit. The important thing to remember is that the amount borrowed should be kept within the payment limits which the child can meet from his allowance. Be careful not to make deductions over too long a period or the training value will be lost.

As with most learning, lectures, explanations, and rules about money cannot take the place of direct experience. It is good to give children the responsibility for spending some of the family budget as well as their own money. Children enjoy paying the bill in a restaurant and figuring out how much should be left as a tip. They like to pay the toll on a turnpike or pay for the gasoline. By letting them help you pay these and regular household expenses such as water, telephone, electric and heating bills, you can help them develop their own attitudes about the worth of various ventures and possessions.

"Consumer" training at home is essential. Children have many opportunities for learning when they are allowed to help choose some of their own clothes and personal needs. They grow as they develop an interest in getting the best possible product for the amount of money they have to spend. Children learn to make choices and perhaps to give up one thing in order to get something more desirable or worthwhile.

Make Children Junior Partners

When they are old enough to understand, it is important to include children in discussions of family finances and methods of making decisions. They are especially interested in choices that affect them. "We can't go on a trip to the mountains this year because we need storm windows for the house." "We must drive the old car for a few more months so that Shirley can have braces on her teeth." Older children can usually be told when the family faces some financial difficulty. However, care should be taken to protect them from needless anxiety. As children hear and share in making family decisions, they learn methods and standards of decision making that will help prepare them for adult responsibilities.

Being a junior partner in family financial matters also means taking a part in the responsibilities of the home. Two common errors made by parents are: (1) giving money or an allowance as a reward for good conduct or normal household chores; (2) taking away money as punishment. Both of these practices associate money with morality. A child's normal household chores should not be confused with earning an allowance. If he is to carry out the garbage, mow the lawn, keep his room clean, and take care of his pet, then those chores are part of his responsibilities as part of the family unit and have nothing to do with money. However, some work at home can be classified as a "job"—usually time consuming "adult" work that the family might ordinarily have to hire someone else to do, or unusual jobs that come up from time to time such as cleaning out the garage. If the child can do these, he deserves the extra money and should have an opportunity to earn it.

Rewards and Punishment

Money is not generally effective as a reward or punishment. One common practice is the purchase of grades by parents. This sort of bribery can easily lead to corrupting the child or giving him a false sense of values. Children are in school to learn according to their capacity—not to win a reward. Grades should not become ends in themselves. Children can easily obtain the desired grades by cheating if the monetary reward is high enough. The same is true if he is "fined" for a poor grade or for neglecting his chores at home. When an allowance is used as a reward or punishment, the educational value is lost. Unless a child can count on a fixed amount each week, he cannot plan the use of his money wisely.

Payment of an allowance should never be skipped without an explanation and should never be cut or withheld, or threatened to be withheld as punishment. Children often become emotional about money when it is used as a disciplinary measure. If money is used as a bribe, threat, or method of discipline, the child may develop unhealthy attitudes about how to get it. Do not put a price tag on everything!

Learning to Save

What about saving? Should you expect your child to put part of his allowance aside each week? Perhaps it will help if you stop to consider why you save. Most of us save with some definite purpose in mind. It may be toward the purchase of a color TV set, for the children's college education, for a family vacation, or for retirement purposes. This is another lesson that children can learn only through experience. In many communities, school savings programs are conducted in cooperation with local banks. These programs combine savings with learning about banking practices. When children discover that by saving some of their cash rather than spending it on temporarily satisfying times, they can buy something better, they will want to begin saving. For a child or even a teenager, the concept of saving for the future is usually vague and meaningless. If parents insist that something be saved from an allowance or earning each week, we teach them nothing but obedience. But if we can help them to plan for the purchase of something definite, and then allow them to manage their own money, they will eventually realize the reason for saving and the satisfaction that it can bring.

Children should also share in saving the family's money. Most of us put money aside with some definite purpose in mind. If the child is included in the plans and understands the goal toward which the family is saving, he will be much more eager to have a part in it. He will discover at the same time that by accumulating his own cash in the same way the family does, he can buy something more worthwhile.

It is important that good spending and saving habits be developed during the early years. Today's youth have an unparalleled opportunity to spend, whether it is money their parents give them or money they earn. When young people work, their wages are usually higher than they have ever been in other generations. Their parent's incomes are also higher. Therefore, today's youth face unusual decisions related to the use of their money.

As children grow into young people they react in many different ways to the nation's abundance in which they share. Many see the empty lives of adults who are supposedly "well-off." They watch others seek status through money. They are turned off by vulgar shows of wealth. They sense that, for some, to shop is not a way to obtain what they need, but a way of using leisure and having fun.

Some young people turn away from a life that seems to be too much absorbed in acquiring material goods. They feel deep kinship with Herman Hesse's character, Steppenwolf, the boy who left the security of a middle-class family to live alone. They gather in communes and dress inexpensively. In urban communes the members usually work part time. In rural areas, some try to live off the land. Their search is for a simple environment in which human beings can be genuinely human.[3]

But to the Christian young person, this rejection of material possessions is just as wrong as the driving obsession to accumulate things. From early childhood it is important to instill in the child a sense of purpose for all material possessions. This is the time to build the foundation on which the rest of life will be built. At this stage the child cannot fully understand the meaning of the lordship of Christ, the Christian "calling" to discipleship, or what is meant by a Christian life-style. But as the child grows and observes these commitments in the lives of his parents, and as they guide him in positive habits of spending, saving, and giving, the child will mature and make sound commitments of his own.

For Your Consideration

1. *What value do you place on money?*
2. *Are these the values you want to instill in your children?*
3. *How do children develop attitudes toward money?*
4. *Do you feel that it is important to include children in family financial planning?*
5. *How is an allowance a valuable tool in a child's development?*
6. *Should money ever be used as a reward or withheld as punishment?*
7. *How can you teach a child about biblical concepts of the use of all possessions?*

Notes

1. E. Nora Ryan, M.D. and Donald R. McNeil, "Much Ado About Money," *Parents Magazine*, May, 1964.

2. Robert J. Hastings, *The Christian Man's World* (Memphis: Brotherhood Commission, 1964).

3. Teens and Money booklet, The Stewardship Education Resources, United Church of Christ by the Stewardship Council, 1970, pp. 4-5.

4. *Baptist Adults*, June 22, 1969, "Children and Money" by Michael L. Speer—much of this chapter is based on material used in this article.

9.
YOUNG PEOPLE
AND
THEIR
MONEY
(Plan Ahead!)

Remember just a few years ago when you thought you would be able to get everything you really wanted—if you only had a little extra money? You probably looked forward to the day when you would have a job, your own apartment, the finest clothes you could imagine, and maybe even a new car.

Well, look at yourself now! You have a job. You may even be married and enjoying two incomes. And you do have more money than ever before. But you are just as broke as ever. Could it be that keeping solvent doesn't depend completely on the amount of income you have? You may be learning an important lesson.

Living Within Your Income

Young people can usually expect to spend at least a few years after they have received their education in self-supporting employment before they get married and start families of their own. During this period it is important to develop good money management techniques. These are patterns of spending and saving that will be with you for the rest of your life. If you fall into the habit of living beyond your income, you will be developing a pattern that will never be easy to break. A responsible person is one who learns early to plan ahead—to do without something now for the sake of something more important in the future.

Sally was going to be a senior in college the next year. One of her friends was trying to persuade her to spend the summer in Europe.

"I just cannot go to Europe this summer," Sally said. "We can't afford it."

"Can't afford it?" Elaine questioned. "Your father is the owner of a chain of grocery stores, and you probably have as much money as anyone in town. What do you mean, you can't afford it?"

Sally explained: "I don't mean that we do not have the money for me to go to Europe, Elaine. What I mean is that I'm considering doing graduate study after college, and Daddy has been invited to spend a month in South America with our missionaries, helping them develop some financial plans. 'I can't afford it' simply means that we have some other things that we consider more important to use the money for."

These four little words—"I can't afford it"—could be the most important four words that you ever learn. As one person said, "It keeps you from eating chicken one week and feathers the next."

Most young people are amazingly innocent about handling money in today's complex world. One problem is that they have not had training in the proper management of their finances. You may be well educated, but you were trained to be an earner. Even with twelve years of high school and four years of college most young people have never had even an hour's training in one of the most important areas of life. Most of them have had very little help at home. They have little chance to get any experience with money management before they are taking on heavy financial responsibilities. They are suddenly confronted with the necessity of providing living expenses, leases or mortgages, purchase contracts, various kinds of insurance, taxes, and many other types of complicated purchases. Financial counselors explain, "Most of the couples who come to us for help have no concept of a budget. They don't know how to develop one, much less how to make one work. They are primarily concerned with living from one paycheck to the next and have no financial objectives or goals."

During a lifetime, well over half a million dollars will pass through the hands of the average middle-class American family. That is quite a fortune, and managing it wisely demands certain skills. Some people believe that money problems disappear as income increases. This is not necessarily true. In fact, the more money you have, the more choices you have to make. With more choices to make, there are more conflicts that are likely to appear. More money requires more careful management, not less.

The Necessity of Planning

Good money management requires a system for planning and accounting. This system is usually called a budget. Many of us shiver when we even think about a budget. But it is important to see a budget for what it is. A budget is a tool that you use as you plan your future. It gives you some direction and helps you do the things you really want to do and accomplish those things that are important to you. It is only as useful as you make it. It must be your own creation and it must reflect you and how you choose to live. A budget will enable you to:

Estimate money anticipated during the next few months.

Determine money required for current debts and for future security.

Show what is available for your day-to-day expenses.

Project your income and expenses for a period of time so you can avoid a financial crisis.

Develop your own spending plan with confidence, being able

to adjust to new situations as they arise.

The most important question that you can ask yourself is "What do I really want in the future?" If you honestly want to have something to show for those hard-earned dollars, you must plan in advance exactly what you want and need. Then you must use the money for those things before it disappears in unexpected ways. Remember that your future is not some far-off point in time when all of your dreams will come true. It starts right now, and you must take the necessary steps to shape that future.

Money management for single people and for young couples is not very different. Virtually the same rules apply. The primary difference is that young couples must learn how to plan together when they are first married—or better yet, during the engagement period. No young woman from one family and young man from another will ever have exactly the same background in the use of money or the same ideas about the use of it. Even after they have been married for many years they probably won't agree on everything. Handling these responsibilities successfully can make the difference between a happy and an unhappy life together. It is important for young couples to learn to understand and appreciate each other's attitudes and even learn to compromise when necessary.

Young couples must face the fact that men and women don't spend money for the same things or in the same way. Each one may think that the other is extravagant in certain areas. When a woman says that she doesn't have anything to wear, the husband may be astonished when he sees her closet full of clothes. On the other hand, the wife may be completely bewildered when her husband walks in with a new fishing rod and reel. This emphasizes the necessity of planning together. When it is necessary to economize, each should trust the other to economize in his or her own way. This problem can often be solved by allocating weekly allowances to be used exactly as each person chooses without any accounting for how it was spent.

Begin early. If you master the art of managing your money now, you will be able to obtain more of the things you want from life in the future, and you will be better prepared to manage the complex financial problems that will face you tomorrow. How you live and how you use your money will be largely determined by your attitudes toward money and how you view its purpose in your life. (The first two chapters deal with this in detail.) Develop your own philosophy toward the use of all your possessions. This will help you determine your primary goals in life.

As with other resources, the Christian young person understands that money belongs to God. God is the owner of both possessions and the possessor, of us and all our resources. God simply allows us to use what he owns. It is this understanding that makes the use of money of particular importance to the Christian. You may have been taught to give to your church from the time you were a child; perhaps it is ingrained as part of you now. But have you ever considered the fact that God may be interested not only in the amount you give through your church but also in how you earn, spend, save, use credit, and plan for your future? A proper attitude toward the acquiring and use of all of your possessions is vital.

A Christian should give testimony of his love for Christ in his spending. Advance planning for what you want and need will help control impulse buying. A Christian should be careful to spend with a purpose rather than on impulse. He should put his real needs and the needs of others above selfish desires.

Single young people and young couples with no children can probably earn more than they need for the time being. This period of life should be used to build up assets that may not come again in an entire lifetime. Remember that life insurance rates are much cheaper while you are young. This is a good time to begin to provide for some of your future plans.

Some young people become upset when they realize that many of their friends and relatives have more money and possessions than they do. It is important to understand that some of these are a little older, may have been accumulating their possessions over a longer period of time, or have been subsidized by their families. The latter is often called the "golden umbilical cord." This may require the young person or couple to live near the parents in the style the parents consider suitable, and may call for paying attention to them socially a little more than would ordinarily seem normal. It is best when you can avoid comparison with others, determine your own life-style, and live according to your own income without envy or outside financial assistance.

Basic Steps in Money Management

The basic steps to wise money management are given in chapter 3. However, these will be summarized here as they relate especially to young people.

1. *Determine your goals.* You probably thought that the first step would be to list your bills. Before you can develop a money management plan, or budget, you must know what you want for yourself or your family. Your goals are the aims and objectives that grow out of your life values. They direct almost everything you do. When you have listed your goals, you have taken the first step toward reaching them.

If you are single, your goals may include future education, an apartment of your own, or even plans for a wedding. Most people either provide for someone or are protected by someone. The single person needs to learn to do both for himself. If marriage is not in your immediate future, you will need to give special attention to personal protection both now and in the future. This will require special planning for health or medical care, as well as your retirement years. If you begin now, it will make your future much more enjoyable.

Young couples must answer many questions for themselves. For example, the wife may have a savings account of her own. The question is, should this money be looked upon as *her money* or should it be considered part of the family assets? If the wife is working, should she and her husband combine their incomes and figure out their spending and savings from this, or should they try to keep their incomes separate and each assume responsibilities for certain parts of the family expenses? If it is necessary for a choice to be made between purchases, such as between a new car and new furniture, which will come first? Only the husband and wife working together can answer these questions. However, if a couple is really to be *one*, it is usually wise for all assets to belong to the *family*. If children are in the future, the couple may decide to live off of the husband's income and invest the income of the working wife as a hedge against the day of increased debts and decreased income.

These are examples of why it is so vital for young people to set goals. A listing of immediate and long-range goals will help provide sensible answers to these questions before they can become problems. Your goals give you a purpose for the use of your money.

2. *Estimate your income.* Do this for the year and divide by twelve to get your monthly picture. Be sure that you figure only take-home pay, after taxes and other deductions. Include other income you might receive during the year such as bonuses and interest on savings.

3. *Estimate your expenses.* If you have records of past spending, they can serve as the basis for this. If these are not available, checkbook stubs, receipts, and old bills will help you in your estimate. List your expenses under two headings—*fixed* and

flexible. Your fixed expenses come due regularly although this may be weekly, monthly, or even quarterly; and the amount is always the same. Don't forget to include your church contributions, an *emergency fund,* and savings as part of your fixed expenses. Giving Christ priority in your spending will establish the purpose for which you live—to bear witness to your faith. An emergency fund is vital. Everyone has financial problems, even the best-regulated families. A frequent example is the problem of meeting unexpected doctor and hospital bills when there is a long illness. But the alert young person knows that these situations may come up, and he does something in advance to prevent a financial crisis. Savings are important if you are to achieve those future goals and provide security for yourself or your family.

Your *flexible* expenses are those over which you have more control. These are items such as food, clothing, and utilities. Although these items are usually paid every month, their amounts vary from one month to the next. Find the monthly average for both fixed and flexible expenses.

4. *Summarize your findings.* Add together your average fixed and flexible monthly expenses. Then subtract this figure from your monthly take-home pay. This will give you the amount you have left for extras. Now you can begin to make definite plans for the goals you have listed. Remember that anything worth having is worth working for.

5. *Record your plan.* When you have determined your goals and established a record of your expenses, it will be necessary to develop a permanent plan for managing your money that can be put down on paper. It will be easier to keep track of this if you use some form of financial record book. This does not need to be elaborate or expensive. You may use a notebook or you can find several types of financial record books in variety and stationery stores. Banks, credit unions, and insurance com-

panies often provide such record books free of charge. Be careful not to make your bookkeeping too detailed or too demanding, or you may give it up without a fair try. It takes practice, but once you have developed the skill, living with your budget is as automatic as breathing.

Keep your budget flexible. There is no perfect money management plan. You will need to revise yours from time to time. It must reflect you; and as your wants and needs change, it must also be changed. As you keep accurate records, they will tell you if your dollars are giving you what you really want them to.

Checking Accounts

If you are not already using a checking account, consider opening one now. A checking account will give you an orderly method of controlling your spending. Making purchases and paying bills with checks rather than cash has several advantages:

You don't have to carry large amounts of money with you.

You can send the check through the mail without loss if the check fails to arrive.

A cancelled check is an automatic record of payment.

Cancelled checks provide valuable records at income tax time.

Basically there are two kinds of checking accounts. These are special and regular. Some banks provide special checking accounts and other privileges for young adults. Check to see what is offered in your area. the kind of checking account that is best for you will depend on how many checks you write in an average month and the amount of money you keep on deposit in your account.

Special checking accounts usually charge you a fee of ten cents per check, plus a small monthly service charge. The service charge is usually about fifty cents.

Regular checking accounts usually have no service charge as

long as you maintain a certain monthly balance in your account. However, unless you write a large number of checks, it is usually better to maintain a small balance and keep larger amounts in savings accounts where they will draw interest.

You will have to decide which kind of account is best for you. Since services and charges vary from bank to bank, and from community to community, investigate several banks in your area and see which offers the best arrangements to meet your needs.

Everyone knows that young people are growing up in a society that promotes buying on credit. Most young people will yield to the pressure and begin credit accounts just as soon as they begin to earn their own money. To get the most from your money, it is important to have an understanding of the wise use of credit. Properly used, this can extend your buying power and give you more for your money. Unfortunately, many young people do not know how to compare finance charges or where they can borrow money with the most reasonable interest rates. If you are not careful, you can "charge it" once too often and find yourself in a financial crisis. A common scene in the living room of many young people is the sorting of bills into two piles. The monologue goes something like this, "You get paid this month; you wait until next." Then they sit back and watch the colors of the bills change from white the first month to pink the second. When the third month comes, it usually brings a friendly reminder which begins, "Have you been away?" Read chapter 6, "Use Your Credit Wisely," for sound advice in this area.

You should also be aware of the importance of some other areas such as saving and investing, insurance, and planning your financial future, including the importance of a will. Each of these is discussed in other chapters of this book.

One thing you already know about life is that it is not static.

Changes occur every year. Jobs change; incomes change; goals change; responsibilities change. With sound patterns of money management you will be prepared to meet each of these changes as it comes.

Your future is *now*. It is already taking shape, and unfortunately this is a point that most people don't realize early enough. You can make it what you really want it to be. You are in the driver's seat, and with a little careful planning you can shape your future to your own satisfaction. The key? "Plan ahead!" You can't afford not to.

For Your Consideration

1. *Why is it important to develop good money management techniques early in life?*

2. *What is meant by the statement, "We can't afford it"?*

3. *Discuss what is meant when we say that young people have been trained to be earners.*

4. *What are some of the issues that young married couples must face when they begin managing their finances?*

5. *List the five basic steps in money management.*

6. *Discuss the advantages of using a checking account.*

7. *What would you say to young people about the wise use of credit?*

10.
PLANNING FOR THE YEARS AHEAD

(Only You Can Make It Happen)

"The point of division between primitive man and civilized man," stated Albert Schweitzer, "is the point where man can give up today's good in order to have something better tomorrow." [1]

The Need for Planning

If we are to have that "something better tomorrow," it is necessary to give attention to the importance of planning for the years ahead. Christian concern for loved ones is probably the strongest motive for practical planning for the future. Everyday life confirms and graphically illustrates the need for families to intelligently look ahead. In one way or another, the future well-being of the family is determined by the plans made in the past. All families are confronted with many needs. Some needs can be anticipated; but emergencies always arise and it is important to be ready for their coming. Many problems such as sickness, accidents, long-term disability, and even death, can be alleviated or reduced through the wise use of our assets.

Here are some specific needs that most families should anticipate and for which they should make plans:

1. An adequate retirement income. Unless you plan for this, it may be a dream that you fail to buy.

2. Adequate income in the event of an illness or a disabling

accident. The loss of income, added to heavy medical expenses make planning for this need imperative.

3. Financial provision for children or spouse. A legally prepared will, a trust provision, and insurance are some of the methods by which you can provide for this need.

4. Future education. Future education for yourself or your children must be planned for if it is to become a reality. Increasing costs make planning a must.

5. Family development is important. There are some things in the future that every family dreams of. This may be a home of their own or a trip abroad. Why not plan to make that dream come true?

6. Provision for Christian causes. There are certain causes to which the Christian family is committed and would like to assist through gifts and bequests.

Some people question whether a Christian should be concerned for the future. They use the Scripture verse, "Do not be anxious about tomorrow" (Matt. 6:34, RSV), as the basis for questioning the use of insurance, investments, and savings accounts. This interpretation of the Scripture immediately brings the Christian into conflict with 1 Timothy 5:8, which clearly emphasizes the Christian's responsibility to provide for his own family.

However, the real point of issue in Jesus' statement in Matthew 6 is one of "lordship" (v. 24). He declared, "No man can serve two masters." The Christian cannot afford to make the accumulation of possessions the consuming drive of his life. Seeking God's will and accomplishing God's purposes must come first.[2]

The Christian family will, therefore, try to live a life that is balanced between being prepared on the one hand, and living by faith on the other. The failure to plan ahead for the needs of the family to the best of one's God-given ability is one way of saying, "I really don't care what happens."

Examine Your Current Financial Situation

On the other hand, if you "really care what happens" you will have to plan wisely for the years ahead. One important factor of that planning is to know where you now stand financially in specific areas as well as in total net worth. Your net worth may be defined as the difference between what you *own* and what you *owe*. Do you know what your net worth is right now? It is important to ask yourself this question once a year. Your net worth provides a guide for your personal money management policy for the coming year. It can help you know whether you should buy, sell, spend, save more, give more, invest, or borrow. Changes in your net worth show whether or not you are making financial progress.[3] It is obviously going to take some time to make the necessary calculations and obtain the current information on these items. Don't expect to do it in a few hours. The time spent will be well worth the effort as the records you will have will be invaluable. The following steps will give you the necessary information. Use a notebook similar to the one containing your money management plans for this tabulation. Do not use the same notebook as this information is only needed occasionally while the money management information is used frequently.

Determine Your Assets

Write the word *assets* at the top of the page. Make four columns down the page and head them as follows: (1) Type of asset, (2) Where we are now, (3) Where we want to be, and (4) Our achievement plans. First, fill in columns number (1) Type of asset, and (2) Where we are now. You will probably need more than one page. If so, make the same headings and columns on additional pages. Your assets will include several categories, and you will need to list all assets under each category.

You will also need the current value of each. Evaluate each category carefully and total the present value of each. Include the following:

Life Insurance. This can be used effectively to provide financial protection for your family in case of death. You need a balanced program. Your insurance representative can assist you in planning wisely. Analyze individual policies to determine the extent of benefits. Prepare a list of policies giving company name, policy number, face value, and current cash value.

Health and Accident Insurance. This reimburses expenses such as medical, hospital, surgical, and related income losses. Be sure that it adequately covers health-care costs in your area. Examine each policy and make a list according to policy number and type of coverage. List the primary benefits of each policy in column (1) and the dollar amount of coverage in column (2).

Property and Liability Insurance. This covers property loss and protects against lawsuits. Protection may be provided by separate policies covering the most vulnerable risks, or a "package" policy combining several types of coverage. Be prepared to present an inventory of lost or damaged property within sixty days of the loss.

Automobile Insurance. List here all policies covering automobiles and other vehicles. List the policy number as well as each type of coverage provided in each policy.

Checking Accounts. This should include all checking accounts and your current balance. Also note here and include any cash you may have on hand.

Savings Accounts. List all savings accounts by location and the current balance.

Real Estate. Describe each real estate holding and the present market value.

Investments. This includes bonds, stocks, and notes receivable. List the number, date of purchase, and present value.

Personal Property. This would include automobiles, household furnishings, and other personal valuables. Identify according to categories and give present market value.

Other Assets. Figure here any type of asset that does not seem to fit in any of other categories and give the present value.

Now summarize your assets. Add the total value of life insurance, checking accounts, savings accounts, real estate, investments, personal property, and other assets. Surprised? You probably have more assets than you thought you had.

Determine Your Liabilities

The second step is to make an analysis of your liabilities. Write the word *liabilities* at the top of a page in your notebook. Make the same four columns with the first one being (1) Type of liability, and the other three the same. Just as you did your assets, evaluate each of the following categories of liabilities carefully:

Mortgages. Include home, automobile, household furnishings, and any other items that have a mortgage against them. Identify each type of mortgage and the total amount owed.

Notes. List any money borrowed that you did not list under mortgages. These would include such things as bank or credit union loans. Identify each and the total amount owed.

Insurance Loans. If you have borrowed money against any insurance policies, include that here. List the company, policy number, and amount owed.

Other Liabilities. Include here any liabilities that do not fit the above categories. These may include such things as charge accounts, and you should list the current balance due. Now summarize your liabilities. Add the total amount owed in each of the categories.

Determine Your Net Worth

The third step is to determine your net worth. This is very simple with the information you now have. Take your total *assets* and subtract from this your total *liabilities*. This is your net worth. (This is the actual cash you would have on hand if you sold all of your assets and paid all of your liabilities.) This is the first step in all financial planning. You can't make any changes in planning for the future until you know where you are now.

Determine Income Now Being Spent to Provide for the Years Ahead

It is important that you know what your future is costing you now. You should strive for a healthy balance between the portion of your present income that is being spent for current costs of living and that portion being spent to provide for anticipated future needs. On another page in your notebook write "Income now being spent to provide for the years ahead." Use the same four columns as before. Then enter and total the income and expenditures according to the following categories:

Income. Include income from employment of all family members, from savings and investments, interests, dividends and profits, and from other sources such as Social Security, pensions, retirement benefits, inheritances, annuities, trusts, etc. Total monthly income from all sources in the "Where We Are Now" column.

Savings Program. Figure and list your average monthly deposit.

Insurance Program. Include expenses related to all health, accident, property, automobile, liability, and other insurance protection.

Investment Program. Identify each program and record the average monthly investment.

Retirement Program. Under this list the following categories: employee retirement, Social Security, retirement insurance, annuities, deferred income, and any other income you can count on.

You can now determine your monthly income and your total monthly expenditures related to providing for the years ahead. Does this reflect a good balance? Are you making adequate provision for those goals that you and your family have set? Only you can determine this as it relates to your own family and specific needs and goals.

Determine What You Want for the Years Ahead

Now that you have a fairly accurate picture of your financial situation, you are ready to determine where you would like to be. Make this a family planning affair. Take into consideration each member of the family and his specific needs and interests. Much of your planning will be based on the goals your family set when you built your budget. Go back through each of the first four steps that you have completed and fill in column (3) Where We Want to Be, and column (4) Our Achievement Plans. You can now make intelligent decisions based on your current financial situation. This will help you achieve the kind of lifestyle you want. It will help you be sure that your dependents have reasonable security in case anything happens to you, and to know where you are going to be next year, five, ten, or more years from now. Your planning should help you answer questions such as the following:

Are we making progress toward buying that home of our own or retiring early?

Have we provided adequately for the children's education?

Do we have enough life insurance, or perhaps too much?

Do we have enough reserves to meet an emergency?

Can we afford that new car this year or do we need to wait? Record where you really want to be in each area you have listed and make specific plans for achieving your goals.

Determine Your Distribution Plan

The family's financial planning for the years ahead is not complete until the total estate and its ultimate distribution is considered. There are a variety of ways to plan distribution, both during this lifetime and after. The overall plan and specific actions related to it should be entered into advisedly. Obtain the best professional advice available. Attorneys, trust officers, accountants, and certified life underwriters are qualified to serve you in their respective professional fields.

Evaluate where your family is now in this area of planning. You have a legal right and a moral obligation to choose the persons and causes you wish to benefit as you distribute your estate. Your rights also include the portion of your estate each person or cause should receive. Without some plan of distribution, the existing law will be substituted for your desires. As logical and fair as the law may be, it cannot make allowances for individual circumstances nor have regard for your personal wishes.

To the Christian, proper distribution of the estate is doubly important since the Bible teaches that all we have to distribute is in reality a divine trust. When a Christian considers the distribution of his estate, it is imperative that God, who provides it all, should be acknowledged. Make clear to your professional adviser that it is your intent to include the Lord's work in the distribution of your estate.

The following are some tools which will be helpful to you in determining your distribution plan. They are discussed in more detail in the next three chapters of this book.

Wills. The will is probably the most commonly used tool for the distribution of an estate. Other people can do much for you but only you have the power and authority to make your own will. No matter how much or how little you have, it is still important. Without one the state will divide property and possessions for you; but it is a long, costly process and cannot take into account your personal desires. Every Christian should have a legally prepared will.

Trusts. Trusts can and frequently do serve families in a variety of ways. A trust can be tailored to fit your exact situation and carry out your specific intent. A trust is a means of placing property or money in the care of a trustee who holds and invests according to the individual's instructions. The trustee pays the income received from the trust to the named beneficiary. A trust may be set up as part of a will, or it may be created during life. It is normally used instead of giving property directly to a person or a Christian cause.

A trust has two main advantages. First, it provides protection of income for beneficiaries who, for various reasons, may be unqualified or unable to handle financial matters. And second, it can assure the continued support of a Christian institution or mission cause.

Insurance. Life insurance benefits make up a substantial portion of the assets owned by many families. It is often possible to provide more for your loved ones and to give more to Christian causes through insurance than would be possible otherwise.

In its multiple forms, insurance allows the family to provide for emergencies involving health, property, and family income. To claim the greatest potential from insurance requires careful planning, and it is wise to seek professional help.

Gifts During Lifetime. You do not have to wait until death to distribute your estate. It is often to your advantage to make gifts during your lifetime. Such gifts afford the personal satisfaction of providing for current needs and being able to enjoy seeing your gifts at work. Also, gift transfers made during your life may result in substantial tax reductions. Consult a tax adviser or attorney for sound advice.

Evaluate your distribution plan. How does it look? Do both husband and wife have a will? Have you remembered Christian causes in your plans? Have you used every available tool for your own best advantage? Make specific plans to adjust any area that does not seem adequate.

Well, how do you feel about the years ahead now? You're probably doing better than you thought you were. With wise planning you can continue to make those dreams come true. You should figure your net worth annually, at about the same time each year. A good time might be at the end or beginning of the year, or at income tax time. This gives you an opportunity to see if you are making progress toward your goals and update plans as your financial situation and life needs change.

One important word of advice—put these records in a safe-deposit box in your bank or some other place where they will be protected. The information from these records is important in case of property loss, a personal injury, or death.

The use of our money indicates what we consider to be the most valuable in the world, or at least the most desirable. It is a great satisfaction to see progress over the years, to watch increased earnings, savings, and investments build toward the goals we have set for the years ahead. You have a responsibility and an opportunity to plan for the years ahead. Only you can make it happen!

For Your Consideration

1. *Name some specific needs which most families should anticipate.*
2. *Should a Christian be concerned about the future?*

3. *What does the term* net worth *mean? Why is it important in planning for your future?*

4. *How does an understanding of your current financial situation help you in planning for the future?*

5. *Why should a Christian be concerned about the distribution of his estate?*

6. *What are some of the tools that may be used in distributing an estate?*

7. *Give two good reasons for distributing some of your estate during your lifetime.*

Notes

1. John R. Crawford, *A Christian and His Money* (Nashville: Abingdon Press, 1967), p. 148.

2. Cecil A. and Charlene Andrews Ray, "Christian Family Money Management," Training Union Stewardship Resource Unit, 1969, p. 30.

3. "Personal Money Management," The American Bankers Association, 90 Park Avenue, New York, N. Y. 10016, 1970, p. 50.

11.
ESTATE PLANNING IS FOR YOU

(Your Will Be Done)

The Christian who is concerned about day-to-day money matters and planning for his financial future, should be just as concerned about planning for the distribution of his estate. Perhaps you are asking, "What is an estate?" Briefly stated, it may be defined as your money and property. When it comes to estate planning, many people think that it is something only the rich need to do something about. They are wrong! The only way to be sure that your family and the causes you care about receive the maximum benefits from your possessions, both now and after you're gone, is to make plans *now*. Estate planning simply means taking a close look at your assets and making the legal arrangements needed to safeguard them now, and later pass them on to the people or causes you want them to go to. Those who do not plan carefully now in light of current conditions, including inflation, will do themselves and their loved ones a grave injustice. In many cases substantial sums of money may be wasted in unnecessary taxes and professional fees.

Estate planning consists of applying your own thoughtful study and the technical advice of experts to the arrangement of your personal affairs and the disposition of your money and property. The purpose is to arrive at the most sensible, practical, and economical arrangements to accomplish what you want. The Christian will not only want to provide adequately for his family but will certainly want to include Christian causes as a demonstration of his continuing stewardship. He will also want to save as much as possible on taxes in order to leave as much as possible for his beneficiaries. The government encourages its citizens to take advantage of the tax provisions allowing them to support their churches and other charitable institutions.

The careful planning of your estate is not something that you can do *alone*. *It requires the advice and guidance of professionals who are familiar with tax, property, and probate laws.* Ultimately, your lawyer will be involved. Assistance will also be necessary from others such as your trust officer, an accountant, and your life insurance underwriter.

The first thing you need to do in the estate planning process is to establish the objectives which you want to accomplish. Outline what you want to do for each of your beneficiaries. Take into account the age and special needs of each of your family members. Also consider Christian causes that you want to remember in a special way. Determine what you would really like to accomplish for each of these.

Your next step will be to talk with your lawyer or trust officer. You will need to provide him with enough information regarding your property and your obligations so that he can get a clear picture of your financial situation. He may ask you for additional information, as needed, so that he can help you make intelligent decisions to accomplish your objectives. After gathering the necessary information, he will be able to make an analysis of your prospective estate. He will also be able to determine how much it would shrink through debts, administration expenses, and taxes. He can determine the net usable value including the liquid assets that would be available to satisfy the shrinkage, the specific assets that would remain, and the amount of income those remaining assets would produce.

Your estate plan, just like your family budget, must be tailored to meet the problems and needs of the individuals for whom, and causes for which you are concerned. Once you know your objectives and the resources that you have available to meet them, you can begin adjusting your assets to meet these objectives. If you begin early in life, it will be much easier to accomplish. If you put it off until late in life, you may find that all you are able to do is to adjust your objectives to the available assets.

There are many implements and techniques available in estate planning. It would be impossible to describe them all here. The use of each will depend on your own objectives and resources. Professional advice is usually needed to obtain maximum benefits. Some of the most common forms are as follows:

Life Insurance

One of the most basic tools in estate planning is your life insurance. (This will be discussed in more detail in the next chapter.) Many insurance companies will provide a free analysis of your family financial protection including projected Social Security coverage, retirement benefits, income from investments, and your current insurance coverage. They can also help you anticipate expenses that should be provided for, such as education, emergencies, mortgages, and final expenses. Adequate coverage now can help ease the financial strain when these expenses become realities.

The use of life insurance is a method of giving that is growing more popular. As children grow, financial responsibilities change. The life insurance which provided security for the family can, in later years, be used to make substantial gifts. Additional insurance can also be purchased for this purpose. Through life insurance a Christian of average means can do something substantial for the cause of Christ.

Life insurance is one of the cheapest sources of money to

pay estate (death) taxes because each dollar paid at death has cost you less than a dollar. These "dollars at a discount" are a more economical way to pay estate taxes than are dollars that would come from the liquidation of the estate assets such as real estate, stocks, or business interests.

Review your policies. You may find that you need to change the beneficiary on some policies or some policies may need to be put in trust to save taxes or to create flexibility. New insurance may be needed to help you obtain your ultimate objectives. Talk with your insurance underwriter as well as your trust officer about the best use of your insurance.

Trusts

For some the establishment of a *trust* may be the best way to meet needs. A trust is merely an arrangement by which you transfer assets to a person or institution to manage for you or your heirs. You alone determine the conditions that guide the trustee. The income from the trust is paid as specified in the agreement. This can be to the settlor (the one making the trust) or dependents during their lifetime or to a Christian cause. Trusts are amazingly flexible. They can suit a multitude of purposes or combination of purposes. With a Living Trust, for example, you can either have the income payable to yourself while you're alive, or have it reinvested for your family's future benefit. If an emergency occurs, you can arrange to withdraw part or all of the money. A Living Trust can include cash, stocks, real estate, an inheritance, or anything else of value. A Revocable Trust can be changed any time before your death. You always retain the right to alter the conditions of the trust.

A trust can also save death taxes and can be designed to permit income tax savings. The simplest use of a trust for estate tax saving is this. You can leave your insurance principal to your wife, but it may be taxed as part of her estate when she dies, depending on the amount of the estate. She could be the owner of the insurance as well as the beneficiary and possibly deleting it completely from your estate. On the other hand, it can be made payable to a trust with the income going to your wife during her lifetime and then pay the trust principal to your children or a Christian cause at her death, and there will be no estate tax. This is just one of the many possible ways in which a trust can help save taxes.

An Irrevocable Trust is one that cannot be changed. These also have certain definite benefits. One Christian lady who was interested in foreign missions, placed $5,000 in an irrevocable trust. She is receiving the income from the trust for life. Since this is an irrevocable trust, she also received a good portion of this $5,000 as a tax deduction for a charitable contribution. At her death the principal will be given to the beneficiary, which in this case is the foreign mission board which she named. This asset will not be included in her estate, thus saving on taxes.

Because of the variety of available trusts, it is important to talk with your trust officer, lawyer, or foundation executive, about those that will best suit your circumstances and objectives. Many denominations have foundations related to their state and convention ministries. The foundation executive in your state, or for your denomination, may provide outstanding assistance in helping you determine the use of trusts for the most benefit for your family and the Christian causes you wish to support.

Gifts

Outright gifts may also become a valuable part of your estate planning. You may give away some of your assets now and take advantage of the generous gift tax exemptions and save on estate taxes later. A man can give away $3,000 to each person or cause in any year without paying a federal gift tax. If the man and wife join together to do this, the amount may be $6,000 per year.

An individual can also make a gift to two persons as joint owners and claim two donations rather than one. For example, a father decides to make a gift of a home to his son and daughter-in-law. If he deeds the house to his son, and the father and mother file split gift tax returns, the father and the mother may each claim a $3,000 gift tax exclusion, for a total of $6,000. However, if the property is deeded to the son and his wife jointly, the total of the gift tax exclusions may be $12,000.

Since your dependents will eventually receive the inheritance which you leave, you may wish to begin giving to them now and thus lower the tax vulnerability of your estate. Again it is important to get professional legal advice on the advisability of this plan.

All illustrations in this and other chapters of this book are given only as possible examples. Always seek professional help with your planning.

Investments

Now would also be a good time to take a close look at your investments. You will want to be sure that these are accomplishing what you want them to now, and will provide adequately in the future. (Investments will be discussed in more detail in chapter 13.) You may find that you need to change your approach to your investments, keeping in mind both your own welfare during your lifetime and the interest of your heirs.

Wills

One of the most important parts of estate planning is the preparation of a legal will. The old saying "you can't take it with you" is true, but you can have the last word about where you want it to go. A will is nothing more, nor less, than a piece of paper, legally recorded and witnessed, which testifies to the owner's desires concerning the distribution of his estate. Practically everyone needs a will. Whether you are a man or a woman, single or married, if you care for someone or some cause besides yourself and want to make your own decisions, you need a will. Anyone who has a bank account, or owns a home or other real estate, a car or other possessions, or has minor children, should definitely have a will. To fail to make a will is, in reality, a selfish neglect of personal responsibility. Such neglect creates a real burden for the rest of the family who survive.

A will is a written document made by you, in accordance with the legal requirements of your state, in which you direct the distribution of your property (estate) after your death. A will takes effect only upon death and may be changed at any time before death. As long as you live, it does not transfer any of your property or give to others any rights to your property. If you die intestate (without a will) the court must distribute your property according to the laws of the state in which you live. This is seldom in accordance with what you would have wished, and the taxes and costs will be much greater.

Sam and Joyce were the parents of two daughters, ages eleven and nine. Sam had done well. He was the pastor of a countyseat church that had grown under his leadership. He and Joyce had bought their own home, built up modest savings and checking accounts and were well covered with insurance. They owned everything jointly and didn't see any need for a will.

The night of their fifteenth wedding anniversary, Sam and Joyce asked a neighbor lady to stay with their children so they could go out to dinner and a movie. On their way home they were hit and killed instantly by a transport truck out of control.

Both of the families stepped in. There were lawsuits and large insurance settlements. There was no will to guide the settlement of the estate or provide for the custody of the children. The court took over. The in-laws on both sides were at first friendly, but both wanted custody of the children. Disputes arose. The judge, a member of another church of a different faith than Sam and Joyce, placed the children in a children's home of his denomination. They remained there for nearly a year before final custody was determined. The estate was drastically reduced by bond premiums and unnecessary red tape. It could all have been avoided with a little careful planning.

No matter how small your estate, you should be completely certain that it will go to those you intend to have it. For example, a married couple with two children may have a total estate of only $30,000. If there is no will and the husband dies, the wife, under the laws of many states, will receive only one-third of the total estate. In this case the children will inherit two-thirds. However, since the children are minors, a guardian will have to be appointed by the court. The wife will probably be that guardian, but she will be greatly restricted in the use of the inheritance left to the children. She will have to provide a bond and she will be under constant supervision of the court. She will be required to file a periodic account of the use of finances with the court. This can be extremely expensive and cumbersome. The children may be denied the use of the major portion of their inheritance during the time when they need it most. This can be avoided with a legally prepared will.

Many people feel that by owning everything jointly they don't need a will. This is not necessarily true. Many people believe that since the survivor automatically receives full title to a jointly held bank account, home, and other investments, the estate is tax-free. However, in the judgment of the federal government and many states, "joint-tenancy" property belongs to the spouse who died first. The surviving spouse must prove that he or she actually contributed financially to acquiring the holdings. If adequate proof of this is not provided, all assets are included for federal estate tax purposes. The assets then become part of the remaining spouse's estate and are taxed again when they are passed on to the heirs. This can shrink an estate very quickly.

Property may also be transferred to the wrong person through joint ownership. If a widow remarries and she and her new husband own everything jointly, her estate may go to the second husband and his children when she dies rather than to the children of her first marriage. There is also the possibility that a man and wife without children may be killed in a car accident. If one outlives the other by even a few minutes, the relatives of the one who died last will receive the entire estate.

It is important to have a legally prepared will. Remember that the laws regarding wills differ in every state. It is important for your will to be hand-tailored to fit those laws as well as your desires. Hand-written wills as well as wills written on forms sold in stationery stores can often bring legal problems. Again, it is important to remember the role that your denominational foundation executive can play as you plan for the preparation of your will. You may contact him in your state, area, or denominational headquarter's building. It is always wise to have your will prepared by a lawyer who specializes in estate work. The cost of having your will prepared by a professional will be minor, and he may be able to save you a substantial amount in later court costs and taxes. Be sure that your will says exactly what you mean. Your lawyer will see that it is stated in the proper legal terms.

In your will you will want to provide for the following:
- To whom your property should go.
- The guardian of your children.
- In what amount your estate is to be divided.
- When it is to be given.
- How it should be safeguarded.
- By whom it should be handled.

In your will you should name an executor. That is the person who will take over all the duties involved in settling your estate. You are free to name anyone you want. You may name a member of the family, a business associate, a bank, or a trust company. This person should be chosen carefully. Do not rely on friendship or family relationship alone. Be sure to obtain the permission of the person named. It is also a good idea to name a substitute in case the first named executor cannot serve. The executor must be competent in his ability to handle money matters. He must also be available when needed. For this reason, a man may name his wife as the executor of his will and name a bank or trust company as co-executor. In this way, the bank or trust company can take care of filing tax forms, paying debts, taxes, and administrative costs, distributing your property as you instructed, or other matters that the wife may not be able to handle alone. Periodically the executor files an accounting with the court. The fee for the executor is the same no matter whom you name.

A will can also make a difference in costs. When an executor is named, you can avoid the posting of a bond. A will can also cut down probate expenses and often save taxes. For example, you can take advantage of the marital deduction which allows you to transfer up to half of your property to the surviving spouse without going through probate. This exempts up to half of the estate from federal estate taxes. When the first spouse dies this can make quite a difference. Life insurance and real estate can build a small estate into one big enough for the tax collector to eye with interest. Every estate in excess of $60,000 is subject to the federal estate tax. Remember, too, that virtually all states levy inheritance taxes.

When your lawyer has prepared your will according to the instructions and information you have given him, he will notify you to come sign it. You will need two or more witnesses, depending on the laws of the state you live in, to see you sign.

After you have signed, they will also sign as witnesses. No one who inherits anything in your will can be a witness. Be sure that the witnesses are people you can keep track of. Their testimony may be needed when your will is filed for probate. If they have died or cannot be located, there may be a delay and unnecessary expenses in settling your estate.

When your will is completed, you may wish to have as many as three copies. File the original copy with your lawyer or trust officer. Place a second copy in your safe-deposit box for safe keeping. Since your safe-deposit box is sealed immediately upon your death, it is not wise to keep the original copy there. Keep the third copy available in your home for periodic review. Don't hesitate to change your will as often as you have just cause. It isn't necessary to rewrite the entire will. It is possible to add a codicil. This is a document modifying, adding to, or qualifying a will; and it becomes an integral part of the will. It should also be prepared by your lawyer and attached to all copies of the will. Be careful not to make ambiguous statements in any codicil that could cause questions to arise when your will is probated. If a completely new will is written, make sure that it specifically revokes any previous will. A new will may not automatically cancel an earlier one.

Letter of Last Instructions

A letter of last instructions is usually addressed to the surviving spouse, and a copy is provided the executor of your will. This letter is completely separate from your will. It is to be opened only upon your death and should include such information as where your will may be found, your wishes concerning your funeral and burial, where all important papers and certificates may be found, the location of your safe-deposit box and where the key may be found, and a statement of reasons for actions taken in your will. You may also wish to include a detailed list of all insurance policies, savings accounts, and investments. The letter is not legally binding. It is primarily to provide information which will make the settlement of your estate easier for the survivors.

Planning your estate, including the writing of a legally sound will and keeping it up to date, is the finest tribute you can pay to those people and causes you love. Don't put it off. Have it ready when they need your help the most. It will tell them, as nothing else can, how much you care for their well-being. But remember, estate planning is a complicated business and to do it wisely you will need the help and advice of people who are expert in their fields. They will help you accomplish your objectives. Don't leave it to chance. Your will be done!

For Your Consideration

1. *What is estate planning?*
2. *What kinds of professional help do you need to plan your estate?*
3. *Why is insurance one of the most basic tools in estate planning?*
4. *How could you establish a "trust" that would benefit you during your lifetime and benefit a Christian cause after your death?*
5. *List some of the reasons why it is important for everyone to have a legally prepared will.*
6. *What is the responsibility of the "executor" of a will?*
7. *What is the purpose of a "letter of last instructions"?*

12.
INSURE YOURSELF AGAINST FINANCIAL DISASTER
(You Can't Afford Not To)

Financial disaster can strike anyone at any time without warning. Fred was a radio broadcaster and frequently broadcast the play-by-play accounts of sporting events. One night he was driving home from a basketball game in a distant city. He had been up since early morning and was tired. He was nearly home when he fell asleep at the wheel of the car. His car weaved from side to side along the highway. Suddenly he awoke looking straight into the lights of an oncoming car. He swerved sharply in a vain attempt to miss the other car. Instead, he sideswiped the car and it ran off the road and into a light standard. Fred was unhurt physically but the two occupants in the other car were seriously hurt. They brought suit against Fred and won a $175,000 damage suit. Fred's automobile liability insurance carried a $50,000 limit. Therefore, he was personally liable for the additional $125,000 settlement. It shouldn't have happened, but it did, and Fred and his family will pay for it for many years to come.

When you buy insurance, you buy protection against financial disaster which can wreck the budget of any family. When many people share in the cost of such disasters, however, no one family has to fear complete financial ruin. This sharing is done through insurance.

Insurance has become one of the necessities of life and should be included as a *fixed expense* in your family budget. This frequently represents a substantial part of the budget, yet it is extremely unwise to be without adequate coverage in several areas. It is now possible to insure yourself, your family, your automobile, your home, and all possessions that are of any value. There are so many different kinds of policies offering so many different types of protection that it may completely bewilder the prospective buyer. It is always best to deal with people who are reputable experts in the various fields of coverage rather than try to master all the technicalities yourself. It is equally important to determine your own needs and buy neither more, nor less insurance than you actually need. This chapter will deal with some of the basic types available in the most common areas and provide some suggestions on the question of "How much?"

Life Insurance

No family should be without some form of life insurance. If the family breadwinner were to die unexpectedly without adequate life insurance, his family might be forced to live in near poverty. A properly planned life insurance program can assure his family of a comfortable living and may even provide for such things as a college education.

Do not take the purchase of life insurance casually. It is such a valuable asset that it should be given enough thought and attention to give you the most effective use. Your life insurance should be part of your overall estate plan. Used wisely it can help you accomplish personal and estate objectives, and at minimum cost in taxes. When you start out in life, your insurance plan will be simple; but as family size and needs change, it will be important to give increased attention to your life insurance planning.

One of the most frequently asked questions is, "How much

life insurance do we need to protect our family?" There is not a set answer to the amount for any particular family. It must be determined by your own personal objectives and in light of other resources. Probably the best answer is, "As much as it takes to assure your family of a normal life, if the breadwinner were to die unexpectedly, or for retirement years." If the breadwinner dies, life insurance steps in and provides income in addition to Social Security and other protection plans to help replace the wage earner's salary. It is therefore necessary to estimate your own family's needs. The following steps can help you decide how much life insurance is needed.

1. Estimate how much monthly income your family would need if you were to die tomorrow. The information you already have in your monthly budget can serve as a guide, but remember that there is one less person and many of these expenses will be less. Some purchases made by mortgage, contract, or installment buying, such as your home, automobile, and major appliances, may be covered by insurance and would automatically be paid for in the event of your death.

2. Find out how much your family would receive from Social Security, from veterans' benefits, from other benefits that you may have in a company and from any other assets such as stocks, bonds, or other investments. Social Security will vary depending on your average earnings covered by Social Security during your lifetime, the size of the family, and the age of the widow and children. You can find out exactly what the coverage would be by calling your local Social Security office. Remember that Social Security coverage will be paid only until the youngest child is eighteen, or until twenty-two if the child stays in school. After that, your wife will not be covered until she is sixty-two, or she may decide to take a reduced coverage at age sixty. This period of time must also be provided for adequately.

In addition to Social Security, check into any additional coverage that is provided by your employer. Most retirement plans carry some provisions for your family in the event of your early death. Figure all of these benefits on a monthly basis.

3. Determine the difference between what you figure your family will need and the amount of protection that you currently have. The difference is the income your family will need monthly from insurance or your other investments to live comfortably.

Actually you will need even more coverage than this, since there are other needs besides monthly income to take into account for your family. An initial amount will be needed to take care of doctor and hospital bills, funeral expenses, and estate-settlement fees. It is also wise to provide a readjustment fund. This should be enough to cover family expenses for one to two years. During this time your wife can be free from financial worries while she decides if it is necessary to sell the house or move to a community nearer other relatives. It can give her time to find a job if she finds it necessary. Also, consider providing for the education of your children.

4. Call in your insurance representative and talk with him about your objectives and needs. Now that you pretty well know what you want to accomplish, he will be able to help you select the best available plans.

Many insurance companies provide the free service of a confidential personal analysis of your family's current situation and future needs. You may want to talk with your insurance representative about this. It will be necessary to provide him with the information suggested in the preceding steps, as his analysis will depend upon accurate information from you.

The next question you will face is, "What kind of life insurance should I buy?" Again, your insurance representative will be able to guide you, but it is important to have an understanding of the two basic types and their advantages. The two basic types are *term* and *permanent*.

Term insurance offers temporary protection and nothing more. The benefit is payable only if you die within the specified period of time which is set in the policy. If you allow the policy to expire, it has no cash value. A term insurance policy is often set up on a five- or ten-year period of time. At the end of that time, it can be renewed, but it will be at a higher rate. One benefit of term insurance is that it can usually be converted to a permanent policy for the same amount without proof of insurability. This can be extremely helpful if for some reason you became uninsurable.

Term insurance provides the largest amount of protection at the lowest cost. This is often important to young people whose earnings are relatively small but who need large amounts of protection while their family is growing. Term insurance may also be purchased to guarantee the payment of a home mortgage or to pay for an automobile if you should not live to do so yourself.

Many companies, unions, and other groups often offer or provide term insurance in the form of group insurance. In addition to your own protection, you can frequently take out additional coverage on members of the family. This is usually one of the least expensive ways of providing family coverage. But remember, term insurance provides protection and nothing more—it does not build any lasting cash value.

Permanent life insurance policies (sometimes called whole or straight life) provide lifetime insurance protection and also include a "savings" feature. With a whole life policy you will pay a fixed premium for a certain amount, to cover a fixed death benefit, and the premium is payable either for as long as you live or a specific length of time (the latter is referred to as "endowment" insurance but is actually another type of permanent insurance). The premiums are lower if this insurance is taken at a younger age because the risk of the insurance company is less and you will be paying for it over a longer period of years. While you are alive, you may cash the policy in for some specified amount. This is called the cash surrender value. Every insurance policy contains information on how much this value would be after any given length of time. It is also possible to borrow money against the cash value of your permanent life insurance. This is usually at an extremely good rate of interest. The rate is also indicated in the policy. The face value of the policy is used as collateral. The danger here is that you do not have to repay the loan on any set repayment plan, and the value of the insurance coverage is reduced until the loan is repaid. It is therefore necessary to discipline yourself to repay such a loan, plus interest, promptly on a predetermined schedule of your own.

In addition to paying a specified benefit at death, and building up a cash value, permanent insurance has other benefits. Many policies will continue in force if you become disabled, without paying any additional premiums beyond those already paid. Although your policy may call for premium payments as long as you live, it is also possible to discontinue premium payments in later years and take a lump sum in cash, a paid-up policy for a reduced amount, or monthly income payments for life. Other family members may also be covered in a "family plan" which combines term coverage on the family along with your own permanent coverage. This covers in the event that the wife should die before the husband and covers the children. Each insured child also has the privilege of taking out a new policy of permanent insurance, without a medical examination, when the term coverage expires or when the child marries, if it is prior to the expiration of the term insurance.

In the event of the death of the policyholder, those who are named as beneficiaries can usually elect to take the face value of the insurance coverage either in a cash sum or as a monthly income for a set period of time.

It is important to have adequate coverage on your wife. If she works and your standard of living depends on her income, this should be covered. If you have small children, you would have to hire a housekeeper to care for them until they were capable of providing for themselves, and this amount should be covered. This coverage may be in the form of a separate policy, may be covered adequately in a "family plan"; or the most economical of all may be to include her in a group policy if such is available where you work, through your union, or other group membership.

Permanent insurance, such as an endowment policy, may also be used to provide for the education of your children. An endowment policy will enable you to accumulate a specific sum of money which will be paid to you at the date named in the policy (maturity date). If you die before that date, the money is then paid to your beneficiary. This kind of policy is usually taken out when a child is young. This gives a longer period of time to build the cash value. The payments on this type of policy are higher than on regular permanent life insurance because you need or want the definite amount of money, with life insurance protection in the meantime, at a specific time.

Gifts through life insurance to your church, denomination, schools, and other charitable causes are growing in popularity. As your children grow older or as you become more self-depen-dent and your insurance needs change, your insurance policies can be used to make substantial gifts. If you feel that you need your current policies for family protection, new policies may provide a relatively painless way of making a significant gift. When the proceeds of a policy owned by the insured are paid to a charitable cause, this deduction is allowed in computing your estate tax. However, if you give the policy to the cause during your lifetime, an income tax deduction may be allowed for the premium payments. If you own a policy already and give it to a charitable cause, the full cash value may be claimed as a tax deduction. If this gift increases the total of your charitable contributions to an amount in excess of 30 percent of your adjusted gross income in the year it is given, you have the right under present law to carry the excess deduction forward for as long as five years.

Some insurance salesmen try to sell life insurance for children. Remember the purpose of your insurance. If it is basically to protect against financial disaster, to protect income, or to provide a substantial gift, the insuring of your children other than in a basic protection policy is probably not necessary.

Health and Medical Insurance

A second form of insurance that is vital to the family is health and medical insurance. This is true especially in light of the soaring costs of doctors' fees and hospital charges. It is virtually impossible for any family to take care of these out of their regular income.

Many companies enroll their employees in a hospitalization program to cover hospital and surgical bills. Others also include major medical insurance plans. This usually provides for 80 percent of all doctor bills and prescription drugs above a deductible amount of $50 for an individual or $100 for a family. If there is a charge to the employee for this, the premiums are usually deducted from the paycheck. If possible, it is always wise to include your family in this protection as you will get the most economical coverage as a member of a group. Be sure to keep all doctor and drug bills to verify your claims under major medical.

If your employer does not offer any of these, find out if some other organization you are a member of does offer such a plan. If not, you may want to ask your employer to consider beginning such a plan for the benefit of all employees and their families.

If none of these options are possible, take out some plan on your own. You should at least have hospitalization coverage.

When you become ill or are injured as a result of your work, workmen's compensation, by law, will provide some benefit payments. The compensation benefits will vary from state to state. Your employer is required to post a notice about them. Know what you are entitled to if it should be needed. Your employer or union may also provide disability insurance to give you some income during recuperation from an accident or illness. You may not need any additional coverage, but it is always best to know the details of all present coverage. If such coverage is not adequate, take out a separate policy for the protection you need. It is usually not expensive.

Home Insurance

In addition to yourself, the largest single investment you will ever make will probably be your home and its contents. It is important to carry adequate insurance; otherwise you could suffer a financial disaster through such things as a fire, tornado, theft, or vandalism. Liability insurance, which protects you in the event someone is hurt on your property, is vital for the Christian who is concerned about the well-being of others. If your home is destroyed by fire, your loss would be only the amount necessary to replace the actual house and its contents. But if someone is seriously hurt on your property, you could end up with a lawsuit and spend the better part of your lifetime paying the damages.

Many insurance companies offer package policies, often called *homeowner policies*, which are designed to protect you against virtually all damage possibilities. These policies are often not much more expensive than ordinary fire insurance and are usually your best buy. Since there are many different types with varying amounts of coverage and covering different hazards, it is important to examine the coverage provided carefully. Policies are also available to cover only the contents of a building if you live in an apartment or a rented house.

As was suggested in the chapter on estate planning, it is important to keep a complete, up-to-date inventory of the contents of your home. This is especially important for your most valuable possessions. One man was asked for a list of the titles and authors of all books lost in a fire. One way to provide basic evidence is to take a photograph of all the rooms in your home. If you have valuable heirlooms, jewelry, silver, or other such valuables it may be necessary to take out additional coverage to protect these. Remember—always determine the things that you need protection for and spend your money on them rather than on nonessentials.

Automobile Insurance

A final area that the Christian cannot afford to ignore is automobile insurance. It is important not only for the financial protection of your own family, but for the protection of others who might be injured or killed in the event that you are responsible for a serious accident. With the soaring cost of automobiles and medical costs, it is necessary to have adequate coverage.

The three basic kinds of automobile insurance are collision, comprehensive, and liability. Collision and comprehensive insurance protect you and your property. Collision pays for the repair of your car; and comprehensive covers such losses as fire, windstorm, theft, and vandalism. You might not need these if your car is several years old. The premium you pay for this for just a year or two could be more than the car is worth. Otherwise it is important to have this coverage to protect yourself.

Liability insurance covers the cost of repairing or replacing the other person's car if an accident is your fault. It also covers injuries to anyone not in your car. Of the three, liability is definitely the most important. It is your protection against financial disaster which can result from a serious accident. It is also a demonstration of your concern for the care of others whom you may unintentionally injure or for their families if they are killed.

Most often liability insurance coverage is quoted in terms of coverage limitations for bodily injury to one person, total bodily injury in one accident, and property damage. For example, if your coverage is quoted as 25/50/10, the insurance company will pay up to $25,000 for injury to one person, up to $50,000 for the injury of two or more persons in one accident, and up to $10,000 for property damage. You would be responsible for any amounts over those limits. If you already have a basic policy, you may find that additional liability protection can be covered for very little additional cost. This is one area that is important to consider. A serious accident may be very remote; but it could happen and, especially if someone were killed, it could lead to your financial disaster. As a Christian you may also feel morally guilty if adequate coverage is not provided.

Saving on Insurance

For the Christian who is interested in stretching every available budget dollar, there are a number of ways to save on insurance. Since these are general and often apply to several different types of insurance, they are mentioned here rather than as a part of the discussion of each insurance area. Consider them carefully and put into practice every one that is applicable to your own insurance program.

1. Compare the policies and costs available from different companies. No matter what a salesman tells you, there is a difference in costs on the same coverage from different companies. Be sure that you are comparing the same benefits. This is more difficult to do in life insurance and health and hospitalization insurance than it is on home and automobile insurance. Also take into consideration the reliability of the company and

the personal services that they offer.

2. Take full advantage of group insurance that is available to you. It is usually the cheapest form and applies to life, health and hospitalization, and automobile insurance.

3. Take advantage of any discounts that may be available. This is especially important for the Christian as discounts are sometimes given for nondrinkers and nonsmokers. Other possibilities include deductions on automobile insurance for a teenage child who has had driver education in school, and certain discounts for "compact" cars or the insurance on a second car. Automobile insurance may also be cheaper if you use your car only for pleasure or drive a limited number of miles each year.

4. Purchase policies with large deductible clauses. Remember that the purpose of insurance is to provide protection against major catastrophe—not against every little thing that happens. Quite often the reduction in the cost on a policy will make it advisable to take a large deductible clause. For example, one company might offer a $50 deductible automobile collision coverage. This means that you will pay the first $50 of damages and the insurance company will pay the rest. The cost for this is $55 a year. You can get the same policy with a $100 deductible clause for $41 a year. Unless you file a claim more often than every four years, you can save money on the larger deductible.

5. Pay your premiums annually. The more often you pay your premiums, the more bookkeeping required by the company. Therefore, premiums are usually cheapest with annual payments and most expensive with monthly payments. If you do not have the funds to pay your premiums annually, put an amount equal to the premiums into a savings account and draw it out when the amount is due. You can not only save toward the payment but draw some interest as well. Some companies even offer a premium deposit plan where they will do this for you. However the rate of interest will not be as large.

6. Begin your insurance program early. Life insurance is much

cheaper when you are young. You can have the advantage of longer protection as well as building larger assets when you begin your life insurance program early in life,

Why Insurance Is Vital

It is vital for every Christian to carry adequate insurance in the areas discussed. It is vital for:

- Those we love to be protected in the event of death.
- Those we love to be protected in times of illness or injury.
- Those we love to be protected against financial loss through fire, theft, vandalism, a natural disaster, or an accident.
- Others who may be injured in the event of a home or automobile accident for which we are responsible.
- For Christian causes which are important to us.

For Your Consideration

1. *Why is it important for the Christian to have adequate insurance coverage in several areas?*
2. *How can you determine how much life insurance you need to protect your family?*
3. *Explain how you can utilize life insurance to provide a gift to a Christian cause and receive income tax and estate tax advantages at the same time.*
4. *Why is some type of health and medical insurance so important?*
5. *What are some of the losses that you are protected against with homeowners insurance? Why are each of these important?*
6. *Name the three basic types of automobile insurance and explain what each type covers in the event of a mishap.*
7. *Discuss some of the ways that you can save money and thus stretch your budget dollar while you provide adequate insurance coverage for your family and those you care for.*

13.
SAVING
AND
INVESTING
(Is It Christian?)

Saving and investing, like every other phase of Christian money management, are related to objectives and goals. Again this involves the life-style which a Christian family chooses.

Most people would agree that saving is important, but some question whether it is Christian to invest. Their argument is that the Christian should not attempt to build financial wealth. That is not usually the purpose of investing. During a period when inflation is running wild, it is almost impossible to just stay even with rising costs.

It is true that Jesus saw possessions as a potential rival to God's place in the life of an individual. This concern was reflected in many of his teachings about our use of possessions. He once said, "How hard it is for those who have riches to enter the kingdom of God" (Luke 18:24, RSV). The god for such persons tends to be their money or even their consuming drive to get money. The psalmist says, "The man greedy for gain curses and renounces the Lord (Ps. 10:3, RSV). The people of Israel were exhorted not to forget God when they had good houses, large herds, and increased wealth (Deut. 8:11).

Today, just as in Christ's day, the threat of idolatry is a very real danger. The tendency is not so much to worship idols carved in wood or stone, but to worship the products of man's technology. Idolatry is not dead—it just takes on a different form.

It remains just as evil—tempting man to let the love of things rival God in life.[1]

There is probably no area of life in which a person's commitment to the lordship of Christ is more severely tested than in his use of surplus. There is hardly anything that will reveal more clearly what kind of person he is. When we have only enough to sustain our lives, our decisions are simple. But when we have enough to do more than simply sustain our lives, the decisions become more complicated and our responsibilities increase.

The responsibilities that go along with prosperity and the consequences of wrong decisions is illustrated in Jesus' account of the big fool with little barns (Luke 12:16-20). Notice that the farmer is not condemned for having an abundant crop or for his wealth or for his ability to gain riches. He is only condemned for his decision of what to do with his prosperity. This man was self-centered—he had an opportunity to help others but he never saw beyond himself. The Christian, on the other hand, recognizes that God's material gifts are to be enjoyed by all. God expects our possessions to be used according to his purpose. When we have an abundance of possessions, or the ability to gain wealth, we have an added dimension of responsibility for service. When we have caught this vision of stewardship, we look out on the world and try to see how its needs can be matched by our own ability to meet those needs.

Saving

One decision that every Christian should make is to place some of his income into savings. In chapter 3, "Why and How to Build a Budget," it was pointed out that one of the three basic reasons people get into financial difficulty is because of their failure to set aside some of their income, in the form of savings, for an emergency fund. To further emphasize the importance of saving, *Savings* was listed as one item under *Fixed*

Expenses.

People frequently ask, "How much money should I keep in savings?" For many years personal finance experts have suggested that a sum equal to about six-months salary be kept in readily available savings for emergencies. However, the most frequent emergencies of any consequence are accidents and illnesses. More and more people are covered by insurance for these emergencies. In some instances, workmen's compensation or unemployment compensation will provide some benefits in such emergencies. If both husband and wife are working, a family would not be completely without income should one of them be unable to work for awhile. Reasons such as these have led most financial advisors to decide that a much smaller emergency fund is sufficient. Two- or three-months salary should be enough for your immediate use if something should happen. It is always good to know that some cash is readily available to meet these emergencies.

Savings Account

There are some values in having your money in a savings account. First of all, the savings account does not fluctuate in value. You are not taking any risk on losing your money. A second value is that your money is readily available if you need it quickly. It is a convenient way to provide a nest egg. In addition to your bank, a credit union is a good place for savings if you have one where you work. A credit union usually pays a higher rate of interest, and often the amount in your savings will pay double if you die. This is another form of insurance for your family. Remember that money in a regular savings account can often earn more interest elsewhere.

After you have accumulated your emergency fund, you can begin to build other savings for special purposes such as meeting your long-range goals. Continue to put some money aside regularly for saving or investing. Pay yourself before your money slips away. Whatever the amount you determine, be realistic in adjusting it as your family needs and circumstances change. Then stick with the plan you have decided upon.

Savings and loan. Many people place savings in a savings and loan association since they normally offer a better rate of return on the investment. Savings and loan associations are financial institutions chartered either by the federal government or the separate states in which they are located. They are designed to specifically encourage savings and to promote loans for home ownership in their communities. When you place your savings with them, your money is lent to people who want to buy or build homes and who must have credit in order to do so. These loans are paid back in monthly payments. Savings and loan associations are the only specialized home-owner credit institutions in the entire American financial system. They are the source of 44 percent of all the home loans currently obtained in the United States each year. Most—but not all—associations are members of the Federal Savings and Loan Insurance Corporation.[2] You should always check to see that your savings are insured before investing in any institution. Ordinarily, each account is insured up to $20,000 by the Federal Deposit Insurance Corporation, an agency of the United States government.

Those who save with a savings and loan association share in the profits made by the association, in proportion to the amount of their savings. This is usually figured each quarter with all of the profits, except those amounts set aside for reserves and legal requirements, returned to the savers and investors as dividends.

Certificates. Savings certificates are also available through most banks and savings and loan associations. These are designed for savers who (1) have large sums to invest; (2) are willing to commit such savings to definite periods of time; and (3) want a high rate of return. For example, you may obtain a four-year certificate that will pay 7 percent interest. The minimum deposit may be $1,000. If compounding is done daily and added to the account quarterly, the effective annual return is actually 7.25 percent. In addition, you may choose to receive the interest check quarterly or have the amount deposited in a passbook account.

Certificates do have a disadvantage. If you withdraw your funds prior to the maturity date, there is a penalty. Earnings on the amount withdrawn are usually paid at the current rate on regular accounts, less three-months earnings at that rate.

Investing

Once you have reached your goal for your emergency fund and have additional savings plans, you may be in a position to begin thinking about investing. Most people invest their money as a hedge against inflation or in an attempt to realize their financial goals. In light of current inflation, your savings account is actually decreasing in buying power. For example, your savings may be earning 6 percent interest, but inflation raises prices by 10 percent. Therefore, the amount of money in your savings at the end of the year will actually buy less than when you put it in, even with the interest you earned.

Investments can usually bring you a higher return in interest and possibly an increase in the value of your invested capital as well. However, you are also taking a risk that the value may decrease. Whatever area of investing you consider, always secure the best possible advice, from as many sources as possible, *before* investing. Investing is a specialized business and the uninformed investor should seek professional guidance. Find out the benefits and advantages of any investment, but also be sure you know the risks and disadvantages. An important word to remember is *diversity*. Don't place all of your investment in one area. The risk of complete loss is far less if you diversify. Spread your investments around in various areas or at least with different holdings in any one area. This will be increasingly possible as you have larger amounts to work with. Don't spread yourself so thin that you can't keep up with all of your investments at all times. Let's look at some of the most common categories of investing.

Real Estate. The largest single category of investment in the United States today is in real estate. One study a few years ago showed that real estate assets accounted for more than 86 percent of the total value of all the tangible assets in the country.

President Franklin D. Roosevelt once summed up a few reasons why real estate has become such a popular form of investment. "Real estate cannot be lost or stolen, nor can it be carried away," he said. "Managed with reasonable care, it is about the safest investment in the world."

Real estate is permanent. It is tangible. You can see and inspect land. You can live in the dwellings affixed to land, or you can use them to produce income. And you know that the land will be there tomorrow, and the next day.[3]

During the past several years, real estate investments have produced by far the best return on the amounts invested. Statistical studies indicate that real estate values should continue to move steadily upward during the coming decades. Some of the advantages of investing in real estate are:

- There is a favorable rate of return on investments in income-producing property.
- The property itself may increase in value
- Federal tax laws contain special features which give extra advantage to investors in higher tax brackets.
- You gain the benefit of "leverage" when you buy property by paying only a part of the total cost with your own cash.

Now let's look at some of the disadvantages of investing in

real estate.

- The money you have invested is not readily available in case you need it suddenly.
- You may have problems managing income-producing property such as apartments and rental houses.
- Property taxes often increase dramatically.
- Real estate loans may be extremely difficult to obtain and usually carry a high rate of interest.

Most authorities agree that a good investment in real estate will produce a 10 to 15 percent annual return on equity, less carrying costs. And for those interested in capital appreciation, they say that it is not uncommon for properly selected land to double in value over a given period.[4]

In addition to investing personally in real estate, you may wish to consider lending money to someone else on the security of a home mortgage. Most communities have real estate firms which will help you invest your savings wisely. Since real estate and mortgage investing is a specialized business, it is almost always best to consult a specialist.

Bonds. If you are interested in placing your money in investments with a minimum amount of risk, you may find bonds to be to your liking. Bonds fluctuate with the money market. If you buy a bond and interest rates go up, the value of your bond will drop, since investors will go elsewhere. However, the interest you receive will continue at the same rate, and you will still get the face value of the bond if you hold it until it matures. However, if you buy a bond and other interest rates decline, your bond will be worth more; and you will be able to sell it, even before maturity, for an amount higher than the face value.

Bonds are evaluated and rated according to quality and risk. The safest designations are AAA and AA, with AAA being the best. The higher the rating on a bond, the lower interest it will pay since the risk is less. Before you buy any bond be sure to obtain a copy of the bond's prospectus. Bonds may be bought through banks, bond dealers, and brokers. They can provide you with a prospectus. Bonds are usually bought in denominations of $1,000. When a bond is a new offering, there is no commission. Otherwise there is usually a fee on each issue. The maturity date on bonds may vary from ten to thirty years, and interest is paid every six months.

As a Christian you will want to know the nature of the business you are investing in before you make an investment. Whether you are considering investing in bonds or stocks, carefully examine the nature of the investment to see if it is contrary to your standards. If, for example, you are opposed to war, you would not want to invest in any company that produces munitions. Or if you do not believe in the use of alcoholic beverages, you would not want holdings in a company, or even a diversified portfolio of investments, that owns a distillery. Your Christian convictions should not only determine when you can afford to make investments, they should also guide you in determining the type of investments that you make. You certainly do not want to become involved in any business that is contrary to your Christian standards.

There are many different types of bonds. One common type is *corporate bonds* which are sold by corporations. These sometimes are available as "convertible bonds." These are issued with an exchange option. This enables you to have the security and income offered by the bond and the opportunity to participate in a company's chances of growth by converting the bond into common stock. The bond can be converted into a stipulated number of the issuing company's common stock shares if this seems more desirable than maintaining the bond itself. The disadvantage is that there is a price for the convertibility feature. Convertible bonds return lower yields than straight bonds, thus you are paying a premium for the conversion privilege.

Municipal bonds are issued by states, cities, school districts, or any other governmental unit. Municipal bonds are issued in two types: *general obligation* and *revenue*. General obligation bonds are the safest as they are backed by the tax base of the government unit selling them. Revenue bonds are dependent on the income received from a specific project. For example, the money brought in from a toll road. Although municipals do not return a high rate of yield, they do offer the advantage of having their interest earnings exempt from federal income tax. If the bond is put up by your state or municipality, there is no state income tax paid either. You do have to pay capital gains tax on any profit you make when the bond is sold. Before you purchase a municipal bond you must decide if its tax-exempt status offsets the limited interest.

Remember that these bonds fluctuate with the economy. Even though the interest is fixed, you may take a loss if you sell before maturity. When you wait until maturity you will receive the face value. If you sell early the current market conditions will determine whether you get more or less for the bond than you paid for it.

Another type of bond that would be of special interest to the Christian is the *church bond.* Quite often a church that needs to expand its facilities will contract with a bond company to issue church bonds. These will normally produce a higher rate of interest than your bank savings or even a savings and loan account. As in other bonds, a prospectus must be provided. Read this carefully. The bond is only as good as the ability of the church to redeem the bonds. Consider both the income and other financial obligations of the church. One protection for the investor is that such bonds must be issued according to the regulations of the Securities Exchange Commission of the government which requires a full disclosure of the church in the prospectus.

If you are interested in long-range investments, church bonds may have a disadvantage. These bonds can often be recalled by the church at any interest paying period without a penalty. This is especially true for local members. In some instances, the bonds may have the benefit of a penalty payable to the holder if recalled before maturity. Church bonds are usually issued with various maturity dates which may be from six months to fifteen years. You may choose the length of time most appropriate to your investment needs. The interest payment may also vary. Some bonds pay interest by coupons which are redeemed every six months. Others compound the interest every six months with the total amount paid at maturity. This actually provides a better rate of return for the investor.

Probably the biggest disadvantage to church bonds is the difficulty in finding a ready buyer if you need to sell the bonds prior to maturity. In some instances the church will buy the bonds back. In others the issuing company may either buy them back or arrange to find a buyer; however, there is usually a fee for this service.

Church bonds are generally a sound investment, and the Christian can receive a good rate of return on his capital while helping further the work of the church. The best source of information on where such bonds may be purchased is through ads in denominational papers.

Stocks. Spendable income in the United States has been more abundant in recent years than at any time in our nation's history. At one time, hundreds of investors with millions of dollars provided the funds that industry needed for expansion. Today millions of investors with hundreds of dollars provide that capital through investing in stocks. When you buy stocks, you are not lending money to the issuing company as you are when you buy bonds, you are in effect buying a part of the ownership of the company. A specific price is set on stock when a company first offers its stocks for sale. Once the original stock is sold, prices are not fixed by anyone. When stock is freely traded on the market, the price changes with supply and demand. The price is determined by what the buyer is willing to pay and the seller is willing to accept. That is true whether the stock is traded on the over-the-counter market or on a stock exchange.

Basically, there are two kinds of stock—*preferred* and *common*. On preferred stocks, the dividend is fixed when the stock is originally sold. This makes the stock company's preferred stock more stable in price than its common stock. There are two reasons that it is called preferred stock: (1) the set dividend on the preferred stock is paid before any dividends can be paid on the company's common stock; (2) if the company fails, the proceeds from the sale of its assets are divided among the preferred stockholders before the common stockholders get anything. Preferred stock holders usually do not have any voice in the management of the company.

Common stock holders are part owners of the company. They share in dividends declared by the directors, receive periodic financial statements, and vote for the directors. These privileges are granted in exchange for assuming a greater measure of risk than either bondholders or preferred stockholders. They gain the advantage of sharing in any prosperity the company might have but they also stand to lose the most if the company does not do well.

Within the common stock group there are various types of stocks. These are usually referred to as growth, heirloom, defensive, and cyclical. Basically, they are as follows:

Growth stocks are those of companies that have the best prospect of increasing the earnings per share faster than the normal growth of the country. They offer long-term appreciation in capital rather than high current returns. These usually involve more risk and greater price fluctuations than some other types.

Heirloom stocks are sometimes called blue-chip stocks. They are those that have paid dividends almost without exception for many years. They represent stock in companies that have gone through times of depression and other unfavorable economic situations and still paid dividends.

Defensive stocks are shares in companies that are apt to do better than average, from an earning and dividend standpoint, during a period of recession. Their main characteristic is a high degree of stability. These can be very attractive when the economy is uncertain.

Cyclical stocks are those which offer the largest gains when business conditions are rapidly improving, but they also suffer the most when business conditions are declining.

As an investor you face two basic questions. These are *when* and *what* to buy. The New York Stock Exchange member firms offer a Monthly Investment Plan that can help with these problems. This plan offers the investor a systematic way to buy common stocks. You can invest any amount from $40 to $1,000 per month or per quarter. When your money is invested, the number of shares bought for you with your payment is credited to your account. Dividends are also applied to your account when they are paid. You may choose to have these dividends either reinvested or mailed directly to you. A plan such as this can enable the small investor to accumulate stock on a regular basis. It allows for dollar-cost averaging—that is, you are acquiring shares through all market conditions and are therefore buying at an average price rather than trying to do the impossible—buy only at the lows. This service is noncontractual, which means that you can discontinue it whenever you wish. One disadvantage is that the MIP plan has been criticized because of the high rate of commissions charged for small stock purchases. You do pay substantially higher brokerage rates on investments under

$100 than if you accumulate cash and then buy stocks with a lump sum.

Another way to answer the questions of when and what to buy for the small investor is to buy shares in companies that own stock in other companies. Among these are banks, insurance companies, and investment companies. An investment company is a financial corporation that pools the funds of many investors to buy stocks, bonds, and other securities. The most widely used is the mutual fund, technically known as an open-end investment company. A mutual fund simply combines the various amounts of money into a common fund, which it then invests. Each investor receives shares in the fund equal to the amount of his individual investment.

There are two values to owning shares in a mutual fund over buying stocks directly. The mutual fund offers professional management of the investment and wide diversification. Most of us haven't the time or understanding or access to all the research that professionals have and therefore cannot hope to manage our stock selections as wisely as those who have these advantages. Neither do we have the necessary individual funds to achieve such diversification.

As in other matters of money management, it is wise to consult an expert for advice. Your most important source of information, beyond what you can learn yourself from newspapers and investment publications, is a stockbroker. Stockbrokers make a point of being well-informed and they will make their information available to investors and prospective investors. They can usually provide "stock appraisals" which are valuable to you as you consider your investment possibilities. In addition to providing you with information, your stockbroker will also execute your order for purchases and sales of securities. In addition to stockbrokers, you may wish to consult the trust officer of your bank or a foundation investment counselor.

As a Christian you will be interested in the possibilities of giving stocks instead of cash to your church, denominational schools, or other organizations. Some people in a high tax bracket may have a stock that does so well that if they sold it, a large part of the capital gain would be lost in taxes. However, they can give the stock to a charitable organization and claim a tax deduction for the entire value. Certainly no one should give merely to avoid paying taxes. But if a person has a strong giving motive regardless of tax considerations, then a stock that has been too successful becomes a way for a person to give even more than he might ordinarily be able to. A person may also have income-producing stock that he really doesn't need any longer for his own security. This would make a nice contribution and again, the current value is tax deductible as a charitable contribution.

Your family should decide what savings and investments are best for you. This will be determined by your objectives. If you are interested in high returns, you probably cannot expect maximum safety on the principal. If you are interested in maximum safety on the principal, you probably will not have protection against inflation. If you are interested in a guaranteed income, you should not expect a high rate of return. The age, size, needs, and current financial condition of the family will all play a part in the type of investment you choose. Remember, whatever area of investing you consider, always secure the best possible advice, from as many sources as possible, *before* investing. Investing is a specialized business and the uninformed investor should seek professional guidance. A professional will be able to help you make selections to achieve your goals.

For Your Consideration

1. *How should a Christian view the accumulating and using of material possessions?*

2. *What are the advantages of having money in a savings account?*

3. *Why do you think real estate has proven to be such a good investment?*

4. *What are the primary advantages and disadvantages of bonds?*

5. *Who determines the price of stocks when they are freely traded on the market?*

6. *What are the major differences between preferred and common stock?*

7. *Explain two ways that the small investor can enter the stock market in addition to individual purchases.*

Notes

1. Cecil Ray. Living the Responsible Life. p. 82 (in manuscript).

2. "Facts About Savings and Loan Associations." Nevada, Mo. 11/73.

3. "How to Buy Real Estate." *U. S. News & World Report*, 1970. p. 9.

4. *Ibid.* p. 19.